# THE DEVIL CASTS HIS NET

## THE WINTER HILL AIR DISASTER

## STEVE MORRIN

**ISBN 0 9534503 1 7**


First published in Great Britain in 2005

Published by Stephen R. Morrin, Stockport.


Printed in Great Britain by
Collective Print Ltd., Unit 6, Guinness Road,
Trafford Park, Manchester M17 1SD.
Telephone 0161-872-1997

We can pull and haul and push and lift and drive,
We can print and plough and weave and heat and light,
We can run and race and swim and fly and dive,
We can see and hear and count and read and write ...

But remember, please, the Law by which we live,
We are not built to comprehend a lie.
We can neither love nor pity nor forgive –
If you make a slip in handling us, you die!

Rudyard Kipling, *The Secret of the Machines*

Dedicated to those who lost their lives on Winter Hill

27 February 1958

They flew ahead of us.

# ACKNOWLEDGEMENTS

This book has only been made possible thanks to a great many people and organisations. I am especially grateful to the surviving crew and passengers: Mike Cairnes, Bill Howarth, Jennifer Curtis (Fleet), Fred Kennish and Norman Ennett for their extensive support and patience with me over the years.

Also, retired Police Officers, Don Hulme, Alan Cretney, Kieth Raynerd and Patrick Wilson. Engineers Alan Sucksmith and John Hall, who were on duty at the Winter Hill transmitter station on the day of the accident and were deeply involved in the subsequent rescue.

I am indebted to fellow researcher Paul Lomax, for his initial help in the early stages of this project, who provided me with many contacts and documentation that were the basis of this book.

Thanks also go to John Quirk and Joe Overty, *Isle of Man Examiner.* Richard Rollon and Jackie Longbottom, *Bolton Evening News.* Peter Trollope, BBC Manchester. *Lancashire Life* and the *Manchester Evening News.*

Colin Owens, who proof read the manuscript - other material was added later and any mistakes found within the text are mine and mine alone.

I am indebted to Trevor Smith for the careful restoration and reproduction of many of the photographs included in this book.

Special thanks go to Sue Somers for her kind permission to tell her still painful story.

Thanks are also due to the following, in no particular order, who also contributed to this book: Ian Campbell and the Ntl staff at Winter Hill, Dorothy Asling, Terry Faragher, Marion Peters, Cliff Smalley, Philip Isherwood, Cliff Greenhalgh, John Brown, Sheila Ashton, Patricia Burton, Dennis Wallace, Joan Halliwell, Sheila McKinley, Colin Ainsworth, Barbara Cursley and authors David Earl and David Hedges.

To everyone I might have failed to mention, my apologies, and not forgetting Lynn, for her support and encouragement during the research and writing of this book.

I ask all of the above to accept my thanks and only hope that the story will do justice to their efforts.

# CONTENTS

# INTRODUCTION

On Thursday morning, 27 February 1958, a Silver City Airways Bristol Wayfarer took off from the Isle of Man with a crew of 3 and 39 motor traders from the Island on a day trip to the Exide Battery Works in Manchester. The Wayfarer was due to land at Ringway Airport at just before 09:55. At 09:45 the aircraft – radio call sign Charlie Sierra – crashed into the north east slope of Winter Hill some 5 miles south east of Chorley, Lancashire; 35 of the 42 on board were killed.

The aim of this book is to give a definitive account of this little known air disaster, which occurred nearly half a century ago; its causes and its consequences, as told by those who were involved. Although the tragedy is legend in Lancashire and the Isle of Man, it was greatly overshadowed at the time by the Munich Air Disaster involving the Manchester United football team, which occurred only three weeks earlier. Winter Hill soon found itself relegated to a few column inches in the inside pages of the national dailies. Only the local press covered the disaster in detail in the following days and weeks.

Researching events that occurred so long ago is always a difficult and unenviable task. I have delved into the local and national newspapers of the time, the Public Inquiry report, official documentation and witness statements. But above all, the personal reminiscences of those involved who I tracked down and interviewed were of the greatest value to me in presenting a true and complete picture of events, and I thank them all. You will find that some of their accounts herein vary somewhat in detail, which is only to be expected after such a long period of time. Nonetheless, that does not make the events described any the less true. I have made no attempt to alter them to make them fit, and are given here unabridged as told to me.

Some of the survivors were hospitalised for a long time and suffered terribly. For the rescuers, relatives and others involved in the tragedy, all were deeply traumatised by the events and still carry those scars and memories nearly 50 years later.

The 35 men who died on that bitterly cold and fog enshrouded hillside were a mixture of experienced travellers and first-time flyers. Most were young, between the ages of 20 and 30. Some of them had never intended to take that flight, but took the places of others, who had pulled out at the last minute. But, through circumstance, once they had assembled together on that cold and blustery February morning at Ronaldsway Airport, they were picked for death. The devil was about to cast his net.

I hope the story that follows goes in some way as a memorial to all those young Manxmen who lost their lives on that cold and inhospitable Lancashire hillside so long ago, never to return home.

Steve Morrin

Stockport 2005

# CHAPTER ONE

# SNOWBOUND

*'They were all very happy and looking forward to their trip.'*
Stewardess, Jennifer Curtis

Remember 1958? It was the year that Elvis Presley was drafted into the US army and Pope Pius XII died. It was the year that Charles de Gaulle was elected Prime Minister of France. The Boeing 707 airliner – described at the time as a 'giant' – went into service, transforming the image and use of international air travel. There were race riots in London, unrest in Cyprus – and on 7 February of that year eight Manchester United footballers were among the 21 passengers killed in an air crash in Munich. But, just three weeks later there was a far worse air disaster, which, unlike Munich, is now almost forgotten in the mists of time.

It seemed that winter was determined to live out its allotted span when on Monday, 24 February 1958, the north west of England was struck without warning by a severe blizzard, creating the worst chaos that had been experienced in Lancashire since the great snowstorm of 1940. Eighteen inches of snow, driven on by howling northerly winds, fell in 12 hours, creating havoc and disruption that have not been repeated since.

The Lancashire towns of Bolton and Horwich and the surrounding villages bore the brunt of the blizzard. In many places road and rail communications were all but cut off and the battle to free them would continue without respite for a week. Trains, along with their passengers, were stranded in snow filled cuttings and motorists caught unawares by the storm found themselves marooned on the main roads. Abandoned cars and lorries only added to the chaos. The whole area was a complete whiteout under many feet of snow. In some places the drifts were six feet or more. It was a freak weather event not easily forgotten by the locals and probably, in these days of global warming, would never be experienced again.

The following morning the population awoke to a scene of desolation. There was no post, no newspapers and no milk. Hundreds braved the snowdrifts and attempted to walk to work. Hundreds more stayed at home to dig their way out of their houses. Then, late on Wednesday night a warm front moved in from the Atlantic, bringing with it sleet and drizzle and creating a dense fog. It was these conditions that heralded a cold and uncomfortable Thursday morning for the inhabitants, but few of them could have envisaged the tragedy to come, which would change the lives of so many for ever.

Some 3 miles to the north east of Horwich on the Lancashire moors lies Winter Hill, which is in effect an outlying spur of the Pennine Chain of hills – known as the backbone of England – running roughly north-south between Lancashire and Yorkshire. At 1,498 feet above sea level, it is the highest point in the area and from the top in clear weather it is possible to see Pendle Hill, north of Burnley, Mount Snowdon in North Wales and Blackpool Tower on the Fylde coast.

The northern slope of the hill drops away very steeply to the village of Belmont lying on a valley floor, which is approximately on a contour of 1,100 feet running east-west. Beyond the valley, to the north, the ground rises again, though not as high, or as steeply as Winter Hill.

It is said that the name Winter Hill originates in the 13th century as 'Wintyheld' or 'Wintyrhold' meaning a stronghold, a place where the local people could repair to in times of danger and drove their cattle. It could also easily have come from the Old English Wynter and Hyll – put simply, the hill that is used in winter.

Winter Hill is a bleak and forbidding place and the area around is steeped in myths and history. Prehistoric man lived and roamed the landscape, as is evidenced by the Winter Hill Barrow, lying a third of a mile west of the summit. This Bronze Age burial barrow measures eight feet in diameter and five feet high and the contents were carbon dated to 1500 BC. Another feature, three quarters of a mile west of the summit is a similar burial mound on Noon Hill, a shoulder of Winter Hill, known as Noon Hill Saucer Tumulus. Excavations carried out by members of Bolton and District Archaeological Society in 1958 revealed the burnt remains of four people and a broken pot urn contained more cremated bones. Also found were flint arrowheads and a sacrificial flint knife. The mound and its contents are dated at around 1100 BC.

Sandstone was quarried from the hill for paving stones between 1880 and 1920, primarily for use in Manchester, Eccles and Salford. The quarry has long since closed, but Millstone Grit is still excavated from Montcliffe Quarry on Georges Lane near the bottom of the hill. Coal was also mined from numerous pits along the summit access road and transported to Belmont, Horwich and Bolton – the last coal mine closed in 1897.

Because of its lofty position Winter Hill was used over many centuries as a beacon – a bonfire lit at night on the summit can be seen many miles away. In June 1977, an estimated 10,000 people gathered on the mist-enshrouded moor to watch a giant beacon fire, one of a chain of more than 100 beacons, as part of a nationwide relay to celebrate the Queen's Silver Jubilee.

Alongside the Pike road near the summit stands the Scotsman's Post, erected in 1912 as a memorial to George Henderson, a young travelling pedlar, who was found shot and dying in a ditch. James Whittle, a 22-year-old collier, was later arrested, charged with his murder and subsequently found guilty. However, at a second trial at Lancaster the jury found him not guilty. It is reported that Whittle subsequently went blind, shunned company and died in middle age. This metal post replaces a wooden stump, which was gradually whittled away over the years by visitors. Attached to the post is a rusting metal plate, which reads:

*In memory of George Henderson traveller native of Annan Dumfrieshire who was barbarously murdered on Rivington Moor at noonday November 9th 1838 in the 20th year of his age.*

During the spring and summer months Winter Hill is a pleasant place for a ramble and provides the walker with extensive views from the summit. But in the depths of winter when the heavy mists descend and the snow lies in deep drifts, it can be a mysterious and foreboding location, ready to trap the unwary. Of these mists there is a local saying, which goes: *When the Pike doth wear a hood, be sure the day will bode no good.* Where the clouds and ground all too often meet, aircraft will come to grief – this is no less true of the high ground of Winter Hill. The earliest recorded accident in the area involved a two-seater aircraft, which crashed into the hillside in the 1920s, midway between the summit and the Belmont - Rivington road.

In August 1942, an American Fairchild Forwarder crashed on the northern slope of the hill injuring its five occupants. Another wartime crash lies just to the north of Winter Hill, on Anglezarke Moor, where a memorial stone records the names of the Wellington crew who perished there in November 1943. The pilot was thought to have lost control, possibly due to severe icing, and the aircraft broke up in the resulting high-speed dive.

In September 1965, an RAF Chipmunk from Woodvale flew into the hill in cloud and, although it finished up on its back, both occupants were able to extricate themselves without serious injury and the aircraft was later removed. The last recorded incident occurred in October 1968, when a Cessna 172 force-landed between Winter Hill and Rivington Pike.

Situated on the summit of Winter Hill is a television transmitting station and mast serving the north west region. Construction of the station building and the 445-foot mast began in June 1955, and on 17 December of that year the last piece of the mast was bolted into place. The first test signals were beamed out on 13 February 1956, and on 3 May ITV reached the north of England from the Granada Studios in Manchester.

Because of the recent blizzard, the transmitter station had been cut off from the nearest access road. On the afternoon of Wednesday, 26 February, station engineers Bob Singleton, John Charlton and Bill Jarvis, the Engineer in Charge, set out to battle their way through the drifts to relieve the crew that had been marooned there for three days. They had only walked a few hundred yards up the narrow access road before they were swallowed up in the freezing mist. On finally reaching the summit the visibility was down to less than 20 yards.

The ITA transmitting station as it was in 1958. *(Ntl)*

After relieving the stranded crew, Bob Singleton, John Charlton and Bill Jarvis, along with another engineer, John Hall, who had been retained from the previous crew, completed the evening shift before bedding down for the night. On the morning of Thursday the 27th they awoke to find a deep blanket of snow and a layer of thick fog surrounding the station. In the warmth of the building they had breakfast, and with the camaraderie that exists on such occasions, shared a joke or two with each other before they set about their daily tasks.

Another engineer rostered for duty that morning was Transmitter Maintenance Engineer, Alan Sucksmith. In 2004 I tracked him down to his home in Cumbria and he told me how he managed to make his way to Winter Hill that morning in the appalling conditions.

The preceding days had seen some heavy falls of snow. Many roads were blocked including the Blackrod by-pass. I had been off duty for a couple of days – our shift rota gave a Tuesday/Wednesday off – but despite the snow some of the main roads must have been passable for I managed to travel from Newton-le-Willows, where I lived, to Horwich on the Thursday morning. Several members of staff travelled by motorcycle and it was our usual practice to leave them at Livesey's garage in Horwich and then transfer to the station transport, a Landrover, for the journey up the hill.

On this particular morning I met Frank Grindley, one of my colleagues at the garage where we joined Fred Peacock, the station driver, and I think Bryn Thomas, the station handyman. We set off up the hill in the Landrover but only got as far as the bottom end of our approach road some half mile or so along Georges Lane. From here onward, some deep snowdrifts blocked the road. At that point Frank Grindley and I decided we would have to walk the two miles to the transmitter station to relieve the engineers who had been marooned there. The driver and handyman stayed behind to try and dig their way through the drifts. I would guess we reached the TV station an hour later, sometime around 9:30am, having walked on bare roads in places but in other parts having to walk through, or around snowdrifts, some two to four feet deep and extending over many yards.

There were now six engineers on site. Snowbound in their isolated and lonely station they would very soon find themselves at the centre of a drama far outdoing anything seen by their 7.5 million television viewers.

**************************************

Some sixty odd miles west of the Lancashire coastline in the middle of Irish Sea lies the Isle of Man. According to legend thousands of years ago, two giants were fighting, one was Scottish the other was Irish. The Irish giant picked up a great lump of his native earth and threw it at the Scottish giant. But it landed in the sea and that mound of earth, it is said, created the Isle of Man. The island measures just 33 miles long and 13 miles wide and boasts a hundred miles of spectacular coastline, many attractive resorts, bustling harbours and dramatic headlands. With its relaxed pace of life, awe-inspiring scenery and unique history, the island is the perfect place to escape for a holiday.

Ronaldsway Airport in the 1950s. *(Terry Faragher collection)*

As Bill Jarvis and his fellow engineers began their morning shift at the Winter Hill transmitting station over on the mainland, a party of 39 motor traders from all over the island gathered in the departure lounge at Ronaldsway Airport. They were all about to board an aircraft on a charter flight to Manchester. One of the passengers, Fred Kennish, recalls how the trip came about:

> All of us in the motor trade were mates. We met each other every day in our work and social life, and for us, February the 27th was to be the icing on the cake – a freebie. Ramsey Motors chartered the plane. They often used to take their customers out for a day trip, and this was just another one of those, we were going to see how batteries were made in Manchester. I was accompanied on the trip with my two partners in the business, Thomas Crosbie and Bill Cain, and my brother in law. We were all laughing and joking when we arrived at the airport to meet up with the rest of

the party. As we walked out to the aircraft I remember someone shouting over to Louis Cowin, who was a great sport and knew all the jokes. 'LOUIS, IF THE DEVIL CASTS HIS NET TODAY HE'LL FILL IT!' It was meant as a joke and we all laughed. Little did we realise that in less than thirty minutes those words would come to haunt us.

Out on the apron patiently awaiting its passenger load was a twin-engined Bristol Wayfarer airliner, resplendent in its blue and white Silver City Airways livery. Carrying the registration letters G-AICS, its radio call sign was Charlie Sierra – after the last two letters of the registration mark. The Wayfarer – affectionately nicknamed the Biffo by its crews – was a passenger variant of the Bristol 170 Freighter.

Development on the type began as a private venture in 1944 to design a simple, sturdy and economical transport aircraft for civil and military use. It featured a large rectangular-section fuselage with two sideways opening clamshell doors in the nose for straight in loading of freight or cars. The flight deck was situated above the cabin and was accessed by the crew by an internal ladder. Although primarily designed as a freighter the unpressurised Wayfarer variant was fully fitted and equipped as a passenger carrying aircraft.

The prototype Mark 1 first flew on 2 December 1945 and became an immediate commercial success. However, the initial success was marred by two fatal accidents. The prototype Mark 1 was lost in the English Channel on 6 May 1949 and another crashed at Llandow, Glamorgan in the following March. Investigations into those accidents concluded that both aircraft had suffered structural failures in their fins due to over-stressing from rudder hard-overs during single engine climbs. As a result, Bristol developed a structural modification for all existing aircraft and the type happily went on flying until 1955 when a West African Airways Wayfarer crashed on approach to Lagos. The cause of this accident, which killed 13 passengers and crew, was due to metal fatigue in a doubler plate in the wing. Once the plate had been redesigned, the wing gave no more trouble and the 200 Bristol Freighters and Wayfarers in service suffered no more problems.

Charlie Sierra in happier times before the crash.

It was with Silver City Airways that the Bristol Freighter found a role with which it was to become synonymous. In the summer of 1948 a Freighter was modified to carry two family cars in the forward cargo hold and 15 passengers in a separate cabin at the rear. On 13 July it made the first 25-minute flight between Silver City's base at Lympne, Kent and Le Touquet, inaugurating the carrier's soon-to-be-famous cross-Channel car ferry service, which proved to be immensely popular as an alternative to slow and uncomfortable sea crossings. By the tenth anniversary of the cross-channel service, its Bristol Freighters and long nosed Super Freighters – dubbed 'Flying Nissen Huts' – had made 125,000 Channel crossings and carried 215,000 cars, 70,000 motorcycles and 759,000 passengers without incident.

Charlie Sierra, the Bristol Wayfarer allocated for the charter to Manchester that morning, was built by the Bristol Aeroplane Company in 1946 and changed ownership on a number of occasions. In 1947 it was operated by Shell in Ecuador and returned to the UK in 1949 where it was converted to a Mark 21 and pressed into service with Airwork Ltd on the Berlin Airlift.

In 1950 British European Airways (BEA) purchased Charlie Sierra to be used primarily to carry outsized loads that would not fit into their Dakota Leopard class freighters, and convey spare engines to their aircraft stranded abroad. However, its career with BEA turned out to be very short lived. During 1950/51 it flew just 204 hours and earned only £9,500 in revenue. In 1952 BEA decided that it was uneconomic to keep the aircraft and leased it to Silver City Airways. The lease began on 10 June 1952 and continued until Silver City bought the aircraft outright on 12 May 1957. Part of the lease agreement stipulated that Silver City would make Charlie Sierra and a flight crew available to BEA at short notice to transport a spare engine to any of their stranded aircraft. In the event the aircraft was rarely, if ever, needed.

Charlie Sierra in British European Airways livery - 1950.

For a short period in 1957 Silver City leased the Wayfarer to its associate company, the Lancashire Aircraft Corporation based at Squires Gate, Blackpool. In 1958 it returned to Silver City and was thereafter operated by Manx Airlines in Silver City livery from Ronaldsway right up to the time of the accident.

Although the Wayfarer was somewhat pedestrian in its performance it was nonetheless a good old reliable workhorse and well suited to Silver City's charter and car ferry operations. In fact, such was the robustness of its design one Bristol Freighter was still in active service as late as 1999 in Canada with Hawk Aviation Services.

The Bristol Wayfarer could not in any sense be described as a beautiful or sleek aeroplane. Colin Ainsworth, who served with the Royal Canadian Air Force for many years, said this of the type:

> During my thirty-six years in the Canadian Air Force I was involved in quite a few investigations into aircraft crashes, happy to say that none involved Bristol Freighters. The Bristol Freighter was operated by the RCAF as well as numerous airlines in the Artic, from the 1950's until the 1970's. Around the time of the Winter Hill accident I was serving my apprenticeship with the Lancashire Aircraft Corporation at Squires Gate Airport, and remember seeing Charlie Sierra on many occasions. During my time there I worked on a few Bristol Freighters and Wayfarers, and found them a very awkward aircraft to maintain. They always reminded me of a World War Two glider that nobody knew what to do with, so they stuck a couple of engines on the wings!

Although Charlie Sierra was owned and operated by Silver City Airways, there existed an arrangement between them and its associated company Manx Airlines, under which aircraft and crews were from time to time interchanged. It was in pursuance of this arrangement that Manx Airlines would operate the flight to Manchester that morning.

Manx Airlines – the local airline – operated some of the very first pioneering routes from the island. Formed in 1947 under the name Manx Air Charters, the airline started operations with two Dragon Rapides and undertook passenger and freight charters to many parts of the north of England, Scotland and Northern Ireland. With the Isle of Man being a popular holiday destination, the airline was kept busy during the summer months bringing holidaymakers over from the mainland. The TT races and the many conferences held on the island also provided the airline with regular and profitable work.

In 1953 two Dakotas were acquired and Bristol Wayfarers were introduced in May 1956. However, before the 1956 season was underway, British Aviation Services, the parent company of Silver City Airways, bought out the Lancashire Aircraft Corporation and Manx Airlines. Both companies were amalgamated to form the northern division of Silver City Airways, based in Blackpool, and in whose colours the fleet then flew, although Manx Airlines continued to operate under its own name until the spring of 1958.

The crew that fate picked out to operate that morning's charter flight over to the mainland were Captain Michael Hornby Cairnes, his co-pilot First Officer William Howarth and Stewardess Jennifer Curtis.

Captain Cairnes was 38; he had first learned to fly, like many pilots of his generation in the RAF during the war. He had some 6,000 hours' flying experience, of which 625 hours had been in aircraft of the Bristol Wayfarer type. Manx Airlines employed him for the first time in 1950. In 1954 he left for 18 months, and then returned. He had also recently been appointed by Manx Airlines as a check Captain. He was neither inexperienced nor reckless. Everyone who knew him would testify to his charm, courtesy and professionalism.

After much searching I eventually tracked down and interviewed Mike Cairnes in the summer of 2002, some 44 years after the event. Now in his early eighties, he told me how he came to join Manx Airlines and his recollections of that fatal flight which would prematurely end his flying career:

> I first joined Manx Airlines not long after they were formed. At the time I was flying for the RAF as a civilian pilot training navigators in an Avro 19. We had to take the trainees on trips for the day, so I thought you might as well take them somewhere nice, such as Jersey or the Isle of Man. RAF regulations stipulated that you were only allowed to fly for four hours, then you had to land and have a meal. So it was on the trips to the Isle of Man that I got to know Manx Airlines a bit. One day they said to me they wanted a pilot, so I offered my

services, and they said, yes, please do.

I started as the only pilot there on a de Havilland Rapide. I stayed with them flying a scheduled service to Glasgow – as many as six a day on a weekend. Then I was offered a job with Shell to fly in Borneo. I went just for the sake of the money really as I was married and had four children to support. Manx Airlines expanded with two DC-3 Dakotas while I was away and Johnny Fisher, a Dakota pilot, joined the company.

Captain Mike Cairnes in Manx Airlines uniform
- circa 1957. *(Mike Cairnes)*

I didn't like Borneo one bit. They had spiders as big as terrier dogs, snakes everywhere and everything you touched burst into life! Then, one day out of the blue, I got a cable from Betty Fisher to say that Johnny had been killed in a flying accident. So I knew about it when Manx contacted me a short time later to say he had been killed and would I come back and take over Manx

Airlines, which is exactly what I did.

On my return I bought a little cottage in Ballabeg – which is now I believe very posh in the new financial Isle of Man – not very far from Ronaldsway Airport. We flew the Bristol Wayfarer's for the bigger stuff and the one remaining Dakota on ad-hoc charter work. When Silver City Airways took over they pinched the Dakota for themselves. But what we did have – and I was sent on a course to de Havilland's to train on it – was the four-engined Heron with retractable undercarriage – a beautiful aeroplane. But in the end Silver City took those too. They thought that we Manx pilots were so used to not having a retractable undercarriage on the Wayfarer that we would forget to put them down on landing! Complete nonsense of course. It was about this time, when Silver City took over and the Lancashire Aircraft Corporation were coming in, that we wondered what was going to happen to us. In the end we stayed with Manx Airlines, thank God, and didn't have to wear their awful bright blue uniforms!

His co-pilot assigned to him that day was 28-year-old William Howarth. He had his first taste of flying with the Air Training Corps, when at the age of 16 he took to the air for the first time in a glider. In 1951 he joined the RAF and was posted to Canada where he learned to fly with the Royal Canadian Air Force on the Harvard basic trainer. On his return to the UK he was based at Tern Hill and then Oakington, where he flew Meteor jet fighters for the remainder of his National Service.

After demob he obtained his Commercial Pilot's Licence in 1954 and joined Silver City Airways flying Bristol Freighters between the UK and various French airfields on car ferry duties. He then spent several years stationed in Ulster in Northern Ireland before being posted to the Isle of Man in February 1958. His logbook showed he had 1,740 hours flying experience, 1,250 of those on the Bristol Wayfarer. Prior to the fatal fight he had flown with Mike Cairnes on three previous occasions –

twice from Ronaldsway to Blackpool, and once from Ronaldsway to Glasgow. Mike Cairnes was perfectly satisfied from his observations on these flights that Bill Howarth was a fully competent and experienced First Officer.

Although Bill Howarth was, in the truest sense, in the employment of Silver City Airways, he was on his posting to the Isle of Man seconded to Manx Airlines under the interchange arrangement mentioned earlier, and was on this charter flight, in effect, an employee of Manx Airlines.

When their flight was called, the 39 motor traders, laughing and joking with each other left the warmth and security of the departure lounge and walked out across the windswept apron to the aircraft. What happened next for Norman Ennett would determine where he sat on the aircraft during the flight and which would ultimately save his life. In a letter to this author in 2001 he described what happened:

> I worked for my father in the family business, which was a garage, filling station, and taxi service. We sold Exide batteries, which were made by the Chloride Company in Manchester. So a day's jolly was organised by Ramsey Motors of Douglas, who were the local agents for Exide. Companies who retailed their batteries were invited on a day trip by air and a tour around the Chloride Works, some lunch and a trip around Manchester, before flying home the same night.
>
> As my father had never flown in his life, and had no intention of doing so, I was allowed to go in his place. I duly arrived at Ronaldsway Airport at about eight o'clock in time for the scheduled nine o'clock take off. As I recall it wasn't a nice day – overcast, showery and cold. Whilst awaiting the call to board I was talking to the Harding brothers who were friends of mine and other people who were connected to the motor trade. Then, just before we were about to leave the departure lounge and walk out to the aircraft, the Captain came over and invited me to sit in the cockpit. I knew Mick

Cairnes very well, as he was very interested in cars and was a customer of ours. Also my wife was a hostess with Manx Airlines and had flown with him often. So I said bye to my friends and departed to take my seat with the crew before the passengers embarked.

The third member of the crew, Stewardess Jennifer Curtis, a young Isle of Man girl – the daughter of the Vicar of Arbory – was making only her second flight after completing her training. Her parents were well known on the island and some of the motor traders on board already knew her. As the only female amidst a group of men on a day trip, she would find herself the centre of attention. She said:

I remember being very excited as this was my first flight on my own – they only needed one hostess on such a short journey. The weather at Ronaldsway that morning was just like a normal February day, a bit breezy, a bit cold, but nothing that would indicate that there would be fog later on.

I stood just inside the aircraft by the entrance door and welcomed the party aboard. They were all very happy and looking forward to their trip over to Manchester – we were to have returned that night. The only passenger I knew personally was Norman Ennett, he was married to one of the hostesses, and because of that Captain Cairnes asked him if he would like to fly in the cockpit.

Once they had boarded they could take whatever seats they wanted. When they were all settled I would see that they were all strapped in – you got the odd one who didn't want to be strapped in and saying they didn't know how to do it, but they were just trying to make a bit of a joke of it. They were all very friendly and seemed to know each other apart from Mr Williamson who was on his own; he sat behind the bulkhead in the tail compartment with me.

For Jennifer Curtis, and others like her, being an air stewardess was something new and glamorous in the 1950s, and it was considered quite something to have landed the job. You had to be in your early twenties, be a certain height, and if you flew on European routes, have a second language, preferably two. There were also strict criteria about looks and weight. They would have about six weeks' training in weather systems, deportment, catering, first aid and what to do in an emergency. With aircraft being much smaller then – which carried 30 – 40 passengers – there was usually just the one stewardess on board, so they were kept busy the whole time, making announcements, serving meals – and if the aircraft had one – selling from the bar.

When Mike Cairnes walked out to the aircraft that morning everything must have seemed tickety boo. There was nothing to suggest to him that the trip would be anything but routine and uneventful when he entered the cockpit. But, by the time he had settled into his seat the first of a number of problems arose, and those problems would stack up as the flight progressed causing a chain of events that would prove disastrous. He told me:

> I remember walking across the apron towards the aeroplane with Bill. I told him to book a flight plan at three five (3,500 feet). As I recall there wasn't a cloud in the sky. When we got in the aircraft Ronaldsway Tower called up and said: 'Sorry Mike, we can't give you that clearance. You've got to go one point five (1,500 feet) for the Wigan Beacon or there will be a long delay.' So we had a quick word with the passengers, to see if they wanted to wait. They said, no, they didn't want to waste the day. The weather looked perfect and I couldn't foresee any problems so I told Bill to accept the clearance as offered. I thought that before we reached the mainland we would be sent up to a higher altitude. I certainly didn't want to go all the way to Manchester groping along the ground.

This clearance at 1,500 feet was made as a result of discussions between Ronaldsway Control and Preston Control; because another aircraft flying to Manchester was due to pass the Isle of Man on the same route as Charlie Sierra at 09:19 at 3,500 feet. The choice for Mike Cairnes was either to delay the take off for 15 minutes until there was sufficient horizontal clearance at 3,500 feet behind the other aircraft, or depart at once at a height of 1,500 feet. He accepted the clearance offered in the light of past experience that he would be cleared to a greater height when he obtained his next clearance at the reporting point on crossing the English coast.

It fell to Bill Howarth, as First Officer, to obtain from the Meteorological Officer at Ronaldsway, a forecast issued at 08:20, of the weather to be expected along the route. The forecast showed that the wind direction at 1,500 feet was expected to be slightly west of north west at a speed of 25 knots. The lowest layer of cloud was forecast as having its base at 600 – 1,000 feet, and the surface visibility was estimated to be between 3 and 6 nautical miles. The general weather was given as 'Cloudy, periods of rain'.

It would have been abundantly clear to any pilot, having experience of weather forecasts and weather conditions, that with such a forecast there would be a possibility of low cloud and mist developing over high ground. But in fact the weather over Lancashire that morning was considerably worse than the forecast issued with dense hill fog, sleet and drizzle over their intended route. After seeing the weather information, Mike Cairnes supervised the refuelling. The fuel he uplifted was sufficient for the 38-minute flight to Manchester with a reserve in case the need arose to divert to an alternate airport for any reason.

There were two possible routes from Ronaldsway to Manchester; one was 'Red Three' which is a controlled airway. It brings the aircraft from the Isle of Man over the Irish Sea to intersect the English coast at Wallasey. The other route, which was chosen for this particular flight, is known as ADR159. It was an 'advisory route', and would bring the aircraft over the sea to a reporting point, some 3 miles distant from Squires Gate Airport, Blackpool. An aircraft approaching the reporting point must obtain clearance from the Air Traffic Controller in the Manchester Control Zone before it may enter the zone. This clearance is given to the aircraft via the Northern Air Traffic Control Centre in

Preston who in turn obtain the necessary clearance from the Manchester Control Zone controller. As soon as the aircraft is cleared to enter the zone any further instructions come to the aircraft direct from Manchester Control. The primary function of the traffic controls is of course to ensure safe separation between aircraft flying in their respective areas. On reaching the reporting point abeam Squires Gate and given clearance to enter the Manchester Control Zone, the crew would set the radio compass to home in on the Wigan Beacon and from there onwards to Ringway Airport, Manchester.

On the ADR159 route, no ground within 5 miles of the track is higher than 567 feet above sea level. Between 7 and 8 nautical miles in a north easterly direction from the Wigan Beacon, lies Winter Hill at a height of 1,498 feet. In 1958 the television mast on its summit was 445 feet high. In the *United Kingdom Air Pilot* – an official publication issued by the Ministry of Transport and Civil Aviation – the television mast is included in a list of Air Navigation Obstructions, under the name 'Winter Hill'. All pilots flying in the area would have certainly known of its existence and position.

Captain Mike Cairnes had flown the ADR159 route a number of times before. On previous occasions he had either flown the whole way at a height of 2,500 or 3,500 feet or, if he crossed the Irish Sea at a lower altitude, he had been sent up to at least 2,500 feet before entering the Manchester Control Zone. Only on one previous flight had he flown the route in good visibility all the way at 1,500 feet. Bill Howarth had not previously flown to Manchester via the Wigan Beacon, but had on a number of occasions flown into Ringway on the controlled airway 'Red Three' route via Wallasey.

Silver City had installed on the flight deck of Charlie Sierra a Decca Navigational Apparatus. This piece of equipment was, in 1958, of comparatively advanced design, which if competently handled provided a very useful additional aid to navigation. It is an instrument in which charts covering the area of the intended flight are fitted, and as the aircraft flies along a pointer, traces its course on the chart with a high degree of accuracy. If the instrument is correctly set and used, the pilot can see, by simply looking at the instrument, what his position is at any given stage during the flight.

The day preceding the flight, R. J. Holmes, an engineer employed by the Decca Navigating Company, had visited Ronaldsway in connection with another installation. Captain Evans, the chief pilot of Manx Airlines, asked Mr Holmes to check the Decca Apparatus in Charlie Sierra. After examining the equipment he found that it was unserviceable and set about repairing it. He took from another aircraft the appropriate charts for the flight to Manchester and fitted them in the apparatus on Charlie Sierra. However, he did not set up the instrument ready for the flight, as this was the duty of the flight crew.

Cabin interior. *(David Hedges)*

When Bill Howarth entered the cockpit that morning he was unaware that the Decca Apparatus had been repaired and was not expecting to use it. When he discovered that it was serviceable and available for use he began to set it up, but for some reason – probably because the flight was running behind schedule – it was not brought into service before take off. In fact as it turned out it was never set up.

With all the passengers boarded and strapped in, Mike Cairnes signed off the load and trim sheets, and with Bill Howarth went through the ritual of all the necessary pre-take-off checks on the instruments, radios and controls. Satisfied that all was in order they started up the two Hercules engines. The 14-foot diameter propellers turned a few silent revolutions before coughing into life. Ronaldsway Tower called and gave them their taxi instructions and the Hollyhead QNH of 1024 millibars. The QNH is the lowest barometric pressure forecast for a given area for a period of one hour. The purpose of the QNH is to ensure that all aircraft, which are flying in a particular area, may set their altimeters at the same standard level. If this were not done, there would be an obvious danger that the safe vertical distance between aircraft might not be maintained. Mike Cairnes set the altimeter accordingly. This setting would continue to be applicable until the aircraft reached the 'QNH Equidistant Line' between Hollyhead and Barnsley, just off the Lancashire coast, at which point the Hollyhead QNH ceased to be applicable and the Barnsley QNH came into force, the crew would then adjust their altimeters to the new setting. I mention the QNH here because it would be another factor in the sequence of events that contributed to the accident.

The brakes were released, and with a burst of throttle Charlie Sierra slowly moved off the ramp 15 minutes behind schedule. The slipstream from the props bent over the faded winter grass on either side of the taxiway as the aircraft trundled out towards the runway. In the passenger cabin the party of motor traders, with seat belts fastened, were in buoyant mood, as was to be expected from a group of men on a day's outing. All were blissfully unaware of the terrible events that awaited them.

On reaching the threshold, Mike Cairnes lined the aircraft up on the runway centre line and Ronaldway Tower cleared the flight for take-off. He advanced the throttle levers and the Wayfarer rumbled down the runway slowly gathering speed. After a seemingly long take-off run he slowly pulled back the control yoke to haul the Wayfarer off the end of the runway for the very last time at 9:15 am.

The passengers gazed down through the cabin windows watching the

Manx coastline slowly slip by beneath them as Charlie Sierra climbed away over the sea as she had done so many times before. But, on what should have been just another one of those routine hops over to the mainland would, within half an hour, change to one of terrible proportions.

# CHAPTER TWO

# ONE SMALL MISTAKE

*'Don't forget the television mast Charlie Sierra.'*
Captain Eric Skemp

Captain Mike Cairnes climbed the Wayfarer to their assigned altitude of 1,500 feet and levelled off. The flight was seemingly uneventful and routine in every way with smooth flying conditions. Apart from a brief passage through cloud in the first few minutes after take-off visibility was reasonably good and if anything improved as the flight progressed. With the aircraft happily set on course Mike Cairnes handed over the piloting to Bill Howarth while he took a back bearing from Ronaldsway, the result of which showed they were slightly, but not significantly, north of track.

On the instrument panel the needle of the air speed indicator quivered around 170 mph as the Wayfarer ploughed on over the sunlit corrugated Irish Sea steadily eating up the miles. Mike Cairnes turned to Bill Howarth and told him to take over the controls as he was going below to check the cabin heating and to talk with the passengers. During his absence Bill Howarth made what he describes as an 'S' turn, to bring the aircraft slightly further south. His reason for making this manoeuvre was that he judged that the aircraft, on its present course, would intercept the coast over Blackpool, north of the reporting point. Shortly after that he set the radio compass – tuning it, as he thought onto the Wigan Beacon, but for some inexplicable reason tuned into the Oldham Beacon instead. Bill Howarth told this author in 2001:

For some reason Wigan and Oldham had a connection in my mind. I'm looking down at the *Aerad Flight Guide* on my knee to find the frequency and call sign. I chose the wrong one, tuned it accurately, and identified it correctly. Subsequent flight into cloud made contact with the hills almost inevitable.

A factor contributing to his mistake may have been that he was trying to do too much in Captain Cairnes's absence. He was, at the time of setting the compass also flying the aircraft – which was not equipped with an automatic pilot – keeping a look out, and also trying to set-up the Decca navigational equipment, which should have been, by rights, brought into operation before departure.

The Wigan Beacon was one of a number of beacons in the Manchester Control Zone. It is a non-directional beacon, which means that the signal it transmits is beamed into the air in all directions. Its frequency is 316 kilocycles with a range of 25 miles and its recognition signal is the letters MYK, transmitted in Morse code. One of the other beacons in the Manchester Zone is Oldham. It is considerably more powerful than Wigan having a range of about 50 miles. Its frequency is 344 kilocycles and its recognition signal is MYL, very similar to the Wigan Beacon. The signals beamed out by these beacons give aircraft flying in and out of Manchester a reference point, enabling them to stay safely on course.

So, instead of heading towards Wigan and on to Manchester, Charlie Sierra was flying directly towards the Oldham Beacon, and that ground clearance of 1,500 feet wouldn't have been anywhere near enough. It would have needed at least 2,500 feet, and even that would have given Charlie Sierra only 500 feet clearance above the top of the television mast on the summit of Winter Hill which had just been built, and had reached a height of 2,000 feet above sea level.

The Wayfarer had just passed the Morecambe Bay Light Vessel and was some 15 miles from the English coast when Mike Cairnes returned to the cockpit and took over the controls. He assumed during his absence that the radio compass had been tuned to the Wigan Beacon.

This was confirmed shortly afterwards by Bill Howarth, who, because of the heavy engine noise in the cockpit, tapped the compass and gave Mike Cairnes a 'thumbs up' when Wigan was mentioned in a radio transmission. Mike Cairnes told me:

> I had absolute faith in Bill; he was a very experienced First Officer. When I returned to my seat I moved the aircraft to the left and the right, as one normally does to check the heading. I noticed the direction of the magnetic compass needle and the course I was steering and to me it looked spot on.

During the flight Bill Howarth continued to make preparations to bring the Decca apparatus into service so they could obtain an exact fix of their position over the Wigan Beacon. Mike Cairnes was unaware that the equipment had not been set up, and assumed that it was working until some time shortly before they reached the Reporting Point. He then noticed Bill Howarth adjusting the Decca controls. Mike told him to leave it for the time being and set it up at arrival over the Wigan Beacon.

As the aircraft approached the reporting point abeam Squires Gate at 09:38, Mike Cairnes contacted Preston Control: 'Abeam Blackpool at this time, estimating Wigan at 43' (meaning 9:43 am). Having received this message, Preston spoke to the Manchester controller requesting a clearance for Charlie Sierra to enter the Manchester Control Zone. Because of conflicting traffic in the zone Manchester offered Preston the clearance: 'To Wigan Beacon at 1,500 feet, remaining visual contact.' At 09:39 Preston passed on this clearance to Charlie Sierra: 'Charlie Sierra, you are cleared to Wigan at 1,500 feet, remaining contact. Call Manchester Control Zone for onward clearance.'

On duty at the Manchester Control Unit at Antrobus that morning was Air Traffic Controller, John Whaley. He said:

> I accepted the aircraft – Charlie Sierra – through Preston Control to fly to the Wigan Beacon only at 1,500 feet, in sight of the ground all the time. The aircraft called that

he had passed Blackpool and his estimated time of arrival at Wigan was 9:43am. At that time I had an aircraft at 2,500 feet, which I wanted to descend to Blackpool, going in the opposite direction. I had through traffic in the area, which made it impossible for me to clear Charlie Sierra safely.

At this point in the flight Captain Cairnes had been fully expecting to be cleared to a higher altitude. It was of course open to him to refuse this clearance if he regarded it as in anyway unsafe. In that event, he would have waited, circling at or near the reporting point, until such time he could be given a different clearance at a greater altitude. He accepted the clearance given to him as safe in the circumstances as they were known to him and his knowledge of the terrain over which his supposed course would take him – all on the assumption, of course, that he was homing in on the Wigan Beacon. Mike Cairnes recalled:

> I was expecting to be sent up to a higher altitude on reaching the reporting point. I couldn't believe they couldn't send me up. Eventually I called up to say I couldn't maintain visual in these conditions much longer, can you please send me up? The reply was negative.

The reason he wasn't given clearance to a higher altitude was because a westbound Silver City Airways Dakota was flying at 2,500 feet and estimating arrival over the Wigan Beacon about two minutes before Charlie Sierra. At 1,500 feet it would be a safe altitude to fly into Ringway provided that the crew had adequate visual reference all the way, that is, they could see where they were going, and provided the aircraft remained on the direct track via the Wigan Beacon. Because at 1,500 feet they would have had probably the best part of 1,000 feet terrain clearance all the way through on the route. But there was very high ground to the north east.

The crew of Charlie Sierra should have been aware that they were on the wrong course, which was some 20 degrees different from their estimated heading. It is possible that the wind direction experienced by Charlie Sierra was considerably different than that forecast, and was in fact a westerly wind, which had the effect of blowing the aircraft north of track. This would have disguised to a certain extent the discrepancy between the estimated heading and the actual track flown. Without the benefit of modern radar and electronics Charlie Sierra drifted further off course, and neither the Captain, his First Officer nor flight controller noticed anything amiss.

When the aircraft was in the region of Chorley it began to run into patches of cloud and light rain. After that there was a rapid deterioration of visibility, and then a sudden and complete envelopment in cloud. Eyewitnesses in and around Chorley saw the aircraft passing into and out of the low cloud base prevailing at the time. They were all struck by its low altitude and the fact it was heading towards the high ground of Winter Hill.

Rain and sleet rattled against the cockpit windows as the engines churned on through the thickening cloud. In the cockpit the wipers slapped hypnotically across the windscreen as both pilots peered out intently for any signs of the terrain below and hoping they would break cloud shortly, but the cloud remained solid. Mike Cairnes and Bill Howarth were wholly unaware of the dangerous situation they were in. As the weather worsened and the minutes passed by the net began to close.

Unknown to Mike Cairnes, another Silver City Airways aircraft, a DC-3 Dakota – Whisky Victor – piloted by Captain Eric Skemp, was making a journey in the opposite direction from Manchester to Blackpool and was tuned into the Manchester Control Zone frequency. What he heard over the radio gave him cause for concern. Captain Skemp said:

> The first I heard of this Charlie Sierra aircraft was a clearance issued to it by the Manchester Zone Controller – 'To Wigan Beacon only at 1,500 feet.' To me that implied an instrument clearance, and 1,500 feet was below the safety altitude for that particular route. It would have been sufficient in visual conditions, and the aircraft might well have been in visual conditions. But I

didn't know this, and I was a little concerned that there was an aircraft flying 1,000 feet below me in what might have been instrument conditions in the immediate vicinity of some fairly high ground and this new television mast.

Captain Skemp's Dakota - Whisky Victor.

At this stage Captain Skemp had no idea that the aircraft belonged to the same company he was flying for at the time. Because when Mike Cairnes first called he didn't use his full call sign, he just used the abbreviated call sign of Golf Charlie Sierra, which could have been any one of a number of aircraft with those registration letters. He also didn't know the type of aircraft, or if the pilot was familiar with the terrain, and that for Captain Skemp started to ring a few alarm bells. He continues:

> I wondered whether I should push out some sort of warning to this incoming aircraft. I hesitated over it because one doesn't normally fly around telling other pilots how to do their job. But in view of the fact that it

might have been somebody who didn't know the area I thought I had better say something. So, just after passing the Wigan Beacon and no more than a minute away from the other aircraft I pressed the transmitter button and said: 'Don't forget the television mast Charlie Sierra.' I didn't receive a reply and wasn't really expecting one. Just after that, the Zone Controller, who might have been reminded of the television mast himself, said to Charlie Sierra: 'Have you checked Wigan yet?' Charlie Sierra reported, 'Negative.' The controller then asked him if he was still flying visual contact, he again reported 'Negative. This of course put the cat amongst the pigeons because the controller knew the aircraft was below the safety altitude. The controller then said: 'Charlie Sierra will you make a right turn immediately onto a heading of two five zero. I have a faint paint on radar, which indicates you're going over towards the hills.' That was the last I heard, because I was then cleared by the Zone Controller to contact Blackpool Tower and I changed frequency and landed at Squires Gate.

Aerial view of the crash site in relation to the transmitter station. (*Simmons Aerofilms*)

# CHAPTER THREE

# THE DEVIL CASTS HIS NET

*'Louis, if the devil casts his net today he'll fill it.'*
Unidentified passenger

The order to turn came too late. Mike Cairnes returned the call with the response: 'Two five zero right, Roger.' At that moment Charlie Sierra was flying above and more or less following the line of the valley to the north of Winter Hill. The outstretched starboard wing dipped in response as the Wayfarer turned onto the new heading. Fifteen seconds later in the course of making that turn, the slope of Winter Hill suddenly loomed out of the white mist. But it was too late for the crew to take avoiding action. Charlie Sierra crashed into the snow-covered hillside at a height of 1,460 feet, and only a short distance from the ITA transmitter station situated on the summit.

The first point of impact was made by the starboard wing tip, then the starboard main undercarriage wheel and engine. The fuselage shook like a wet dog as it bounced across the hillside with mud and snow exploding over the cabin windows. The Wayfarer then began to cartwheel uncontrollably, disintegrating as it ploughed forwards and upwards for 260 yards towards the summit. Both engines were ripped from their mountings followed by the wings. As the aircraft broke up the cockpit was torn away from the main fuselage, bounced and turned over and hit the ground inverted. The tail section also broke away and ploughed on, slewing round to face the direction of flight before coming to an abrupt stop, its silver-grey tail fin upright and defiant against the violent assault.

When the remains of the shattered airliner finally came to rest, the scene was ghastly. The litter of the wreckage was strewn in a long trail across the hillside, the snow stained yellow from the spilt fuel from the ruptured tanks. The two engines with twisted propellers lay cold and silent only yards from each other; one was almost buried in the peat, the other crushing a passenger beneath. Scattered all around were the mutilated bodies of the dead, their personal belongings, hand luggage and bright yellow life jackets – some neatly folded and some partly inflated. Near the crown of the hill were larger pieces of aluminium sheeting, bending back in the breeze. All around the wreckage field the overpowering smell of aviation fuel hung heavily in the thickening mist, but thankfully there was no explosion or fire. An eerie silence pervaded over the scene; there were no calls of distress, just the sigh of the wind over desolate moorland. Some distance from the main wreckage a man's pocket watch lay in a pillow of undisturbed snow – it had stopped at 9:45.

Working alongside John Whaley at the Manchester Control Unit was Maurice Ladd, the radar operator responsible for tracking Charlie Sierra into the Manchester Control Zone. He said:

> I was looking at the radar screen when I caught sight of a faint echo of the aircraft, which would not normally be within range of the equipment in that position. I realised it was over Chorley instead of the Wigan Radio Beacon, where it should have been at that time. I immediately informed the pilot that he should turn right in a direction of 250 degrees, as I thought I had seen on the radar that it was heading towards the hills. His reply was '250 degrees Roger,' meaning that the aircraft had received my instructions. There were only three faint echoes on the screen before they disappeared altogether. There were about twenty five seconds between its appearing and disappearing.

> Then other aircraft were calling on that frequency, and I called Charlie Sierra as soon as possible for transmission, to ascertain if he was proceeding as

instructed. No reply was received and I broadcast to him to climb immediately to 2,500 feet. These instructions were not acknowledged and other aircraft on the same frequency attempted also to relay the instruction, without success. The time then was about 9:46 am.

Manchester Control continued to call the aircraft at intervals, but no reply was received and soon afterwards ascertained the aircraft was lost, presumed crashed in the neighbourhood of Winter Hill.

Amongst all the dead instruments in the shattered upturned cockpit, only the ticking of the onboard clock broke the cold deathly silence, somehow having survived the violence of the crash.

Mike Cairnes described to me the final moments of the flight and the impact:

> Suddenly we seemed to run out of the cloud and there was a certain amount of visibility – I suppose the mountain lifted it a bit. Then I remember seeing a flat area of land and the hillside ahead. But it was too late; we hit the higher ground – there was no shocks or bumps. I saw the starboard engine come out of the wing dragging its entrains and I just had time to turn and look out of the other window and see the port engine coming out – then I became unconscious.
>
> I came round almost immediately after the cockpit section came to rest inverted. I had no pain whatsoever – nothing. I put my hand up to my face because I couldn't see. Oh my God, I thought, I'm blind – I've always dreaded blindness. Then I realised I had a gash across my forehead and there was a huge flap of skin hanging down over my eyes and that was why I couldn't see. I pushed the flap up and held it with my hand. I turned to Bill and said: 'Bill, can you get me my hat, it's over there, I can see it?' He passed me the hat and I put it on over the flap of skin to hold it up so that I could see.

Then I saw my shoe. My God, I thought, my left foot is still in it! I asked Bill to pass me that too. It was still just about connected to my leg by a few entrails. I had fibulas and tibias and everything else sticking out of my legs, but strangely at the time I didn't feel a thing – shock you know. I remember holding the shoe with my foot in it against my chest right until the time I was rescued and taken to hospital.

Air accident investigators examine the upturned cockpit. *(Fred Kennish)*

Bill asked me if the radio compass had shown we had passed the Wigan Beacon. I said, 'Definitely no.' I asked him to try the aircraft radio to call Manchester and summon help, but he said it was smashed.

For First Officer Bill Howarth the crash came with little warning. Immediately after the cockpit came to rest inverted he found himself suspended upside down by his seat harness with blood pouring from a head wound. He recalled:

We hit the ground and there was a series of hard bumps. I remember a split second glimpse of snow through my windscreen – I was seeing the hillside as the aircraft cartwheeled. The aircraft then began to break up, the nose section broke away and bounced into the air, turning over on its back – I was conscious the whole time. When we came to rest I untied my strap and fell onto the roof. Mike Cairnes was disabled in his seat. I pulled him half way out through the emergency hatch in the cockpit roof but he was in great pain. I could see that I couldn't manage on my own so I told Mike I would attend to the passengers and get help. I climbed the crew ladder and on looking back found that the aircraft had completely broken up and most of the passengers seemed to be dead.

Norman Ennett, the passenger who occupied the jump seat behind the crew in the cockpit told me:

Before we took off from Ronaldsway, Captain Cairnes gave me a headset to wear so I could hear what was going on during the flight. But there was so much crackling and interference on the radio that I didn't understand much of the conversation. We took off and Mike Cairnes told me we were going to fly air to ground, which I understood to mean keeping the ground in sight at 1,500 feet.

Visibility was pretty poor when we arrived over England and we soon lost contact with the ground. The next thing I remember is picking myself up off the cockpit roof – my seat belt had broken – and Mike asking me if I was all right. There was a big gapping hole on the right hand side. I remember Bill Howarth was standing outside and saying to Mike what a mess it all was. He said there was a path or track in the snow and he would try and find help. I offered to go with him but he told me it was snowing and to stay under cover

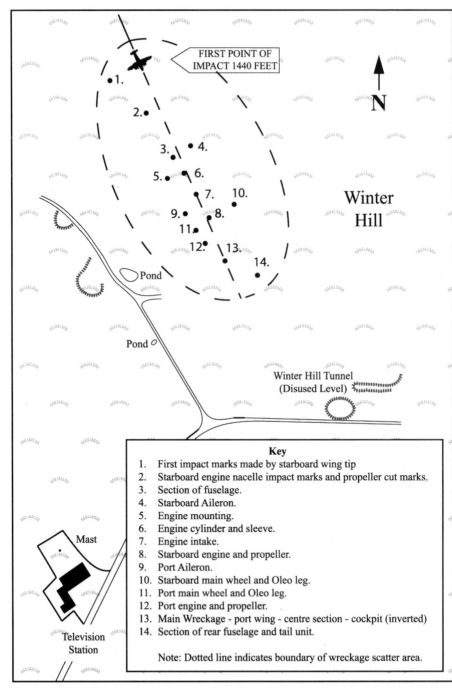

**FIRST POINT OF IMPACT 1440 FEET**

N

Winter Hill

Pond

Pond

Winter Hill Tunnel
(Disused Level)

Mast

Television Station

**Key**

1. First impact marks made by starboard wing tip
2. Starboard engine nacelle impact marks and propeller cut marks.
3. Section of fuselage.
4. Starboard Aileron.
5. Engine mounting.
6. Engine cylinder and sleeve.
7. Engine intake.
8. Starboard engine and propeller.
9. Port Aileron.
10. Starboard main wheel and Oleo leg.
11. Port main wheel and Oleo leg.
12. Port engine and propeller.
13. Main Wreckage - port wing - centre section - cockpit (inverted)
14. Section of rear fuselage and tail unit.

Note: Dotted line indicates boundary of wreckage scatter area.

**LOCATION OF ACCIDENT SITE IN RELATION TO THE TRANSMITTER STATION**

and try and help Mike.

My left shoulder and arm were very sore and just hanging down by my side. I had a piece of Perspex from the shattered windshield embedded in my temple just above my right eye and blood trickling down my face. Somehow in the crash I had lost my left shoe and wristwatch. I looked very hard for them but never found either.

For Bill Howarth, it must have been a devastating sight perched atop the ladder looking back down the slope at that ghastly scene of carnage. Seeing that chaos of twisted metal that was once the passenger cabin, and the scattered bodies of the dead, he must have despaired that anyone had survived. In desperation he called out to Jennifer Curtis, and on hearing a muffled reply somewhere in the mist, set off up the slope weaving between the wreckage towards the tail section.

The crash site shows the complete disintegration of the passenger cabin. *(Author's collection)*

Jennifer Curtis recalled to this author her recollections of the last part of the flight and the moment of impact and the subsequent aftermath:

The crash came as a complete surprise to us all. Soon after we became airborne I informed the passengers that they could unfasten their safety belts, and they could smoke if they so wished. I then regulated the heating arrangements. I remember walking up and down the aisle, speaking to passengers who wanted to talk with me, and asking others if they were comfortable – you get to know when to break off and return to your own seat. I had decided that as the passengers were quite happy and chatting away with each other, I would make up the trim sheet for the return trip which was part of my duties – the trim sheet being the total all up weight of the aircraft. I sat there with this pad of graph paper and it was coming along very nicely. We were always told to do it in pencil so that if we made a mistake we could easily correct it. But on this day I did it in a biro. Then suddenly I felt this bump and the pen went up in an arc across the sheet – that was the moment of impact. But I was more concerned at the time about having made this error. I just remember thinking to myself – I've spoilt it, and now I'm going to have to do it again, had I done it in pencil this would not have happened. I glanced quickly at my watch and it was 9:40. I then felt myself being hurled through the air and then blacking out.

When I came round I just slowly opened my eyes, and to my utter amazement found myself lying face down in very deep soft snow. I thought this couldn't be true, I must be dreaming. I'll shut my eyes and when I open them again I'll be back in the aircraft. But I wasn't dreaming. We had crashed.

I looked at my watch and it was 9:50, so from the moment of the first impact to my recovering consciousness it was only ten minutes. I looked around and I could see swirling mist and tendrils of fog coming towards me. I felt extremely lonely and a little bit frightened, only because I couldn't see anybody else alive. I realised I was on top of a mountain and wondered where I was. When I looked around and really got my eyes in focus, I could see a semicircle of very badly mutilated passengers. I could see from their horrific injuries that they were definitely dead – they couldn't possibly be alive.

I was now starting to feel very cold. In a state of shock I made my way to the tail section – which was the only piece of the aircraft still intact – and sat in my seat more or less to gather my thoughts and work out what I was going to do next. Then I heard Bill Howarth's voice through the mist calling out my name. I stood up and called back to him. Eventually he appeared out of the mist and made his way over to the tail and said – 'Thank God you're alive.' He asked me how I was; I said I was extremely cold. He seemed to be holding onto one huge glove – like a gauntlet – so he gave me that to put on. He said he was going to get help. I wanted to go with him, but he told me to wait in the aircraft, which I found a bit daunting. In the meantime Mr Williamson appeared from somewhere and we both sat in our seats waiting for help to arrive.

In the crash I had lost my shoes, very expensive shoes, I remember being very annoyed about that and my feet were now terribly cold. In the aircraft I found two unused sick bags and placed them on my feet because they were so cold, I think Mr Williamson did the same, he had lost at least one shoe.

Harold Williamson's survival was fortuitous, in that he was seated behind the bulkhead in the tail section with the stewardess. Shortly after the crash he gave the following account to the air accident investigators:

I occupied the front seat of the rear compartment on the right hand side, immediately behind the bulkhead. There were two seats behind me, which were occupied when I boarded the plane, but during the flight they moved forward to the front with the rest of the party. Apart from the stewardess, I was the only passenger in the tail section.

We had a smooth trip over the sea and crossed the coast near Blackpool. As we flew inland I was looking at the snow on the ground. We then started to run into patches of cloud, and within two or three minutes the visibility was nil. I stopped looking out of the window, took my cap off, and settled myself comfortably in my seat.

We had only been flying in cloud for a few minutes when there was a heavy bump – then another more violent bump. I then found myself thrown forward with my head pushed against the rear bulkhead in a crouched position. Out of the corner of my eye I seemed to see my window vanish and a shower of snow and mud streaming past me. We hurtled along in a straight line in these conditions for a few seconds before we came to an abrupt stop, the tail swinging to one side. I was somersaulted across the cabin curled into a ball, landing upside down with my back against the entrance door.

I don't think the crash was as bad as coming off at Windy at 90 [Windy Corner, a notorious bend on the TT course] – it was over that quick. Everything was now very quiet. I managed to get up and stood up as straight as I could, I was pretty sore and couldn't breathe very deep. On looking towards the bulkhead I saw nothing but mist and snow. There was no sign of the rest of the plane other than a piece of one wing. I saw Miss Curtis sitting in her seat holding her hands over her face, which was streaming with blood, she was dreadfully shocked although not badly hurt. I said to her, 'We've crashed somewhere.' I then sat down in the remains of my seat to try and collect myself. Whilst I was sitting there the First Officer appeared, running out of the mist. He climbed into the tail and took the first aid box out of the cupboard and offered it to us. He looked at the stewardess and told her she had cuts to her nose andmouth. He said: 'I don't think there is anything I can do for anyone outside. They all appear to be dead. I am going to look for help.'

I then got out of the plane and hobbled around as well as I could to see if anyone was alive. All the bodies I came across were covered with blood. I found one person breathing heavily, but I was unable to identify him. I then came across a second man still alive (Fred Kennish) he kept repeating the name 'Connie.' I then circled the tail section and found another survivor; he was propped up on one elbow. He said to me: 'Where are we?' I replied that I didn't know and asked him if he was badly hurt. He said he thought he had a broken leg and his stomach was very sore. I tried to find something to cover him to keep him warm but there was nothing big enough and I couldn't stoop down to him. He said to leave him, as he was quite comfortable, which I thought a bit of an exaggeration, as I was hellish uncomfortable and cold. There was nothing more I could do for them so I returned to my seat in the tail and stayed with Miss Curtis waiting for help to arrive.

Fred Kennish, who was seated half way down the cabin on the left hand side, was hurled violently through the fuselage as the aircraft disintegrated. Suffering from multiple injuries he was initially left for dead at the scene. He told me:

When we passed over Blackpool the visibility was very good. I could clearly see the damage to the pier, which had recently been on fire. The last thing I remember is taking a puff on my cigarette, and that was it. It all happened so quickly I never felt a jerk or a bump. I thank God for taking that moment out of my life. I kept my seat belt on during the flight – no reason really – but it saved me. Otherwise I would have gone through the roof. I don't remember anything else until I found myself lying in the snow shouting my wife's name – 'Connie.' – and even then I didn't know that there had been an accident.

The tail section looms out of the mist. *(Author's collection)*

His business partner, Thomas Crosbie, who was seated directly in front of Fred, said in his written statement shortly after the crash:

During the early part of the flight I was reading the newspaper. When we were passing over Blackpool, Fred leaned over and drew my attention to the pier, and at that time the visibility was very good. As we flew inland, I looked out of the window and saw that the visibility was now nil – I remarked on this to Bill Cain who was sat next to me. Shortly after that I fell asleep. I awoke to find myself lying on the ground in the snow and Harold Williamson, one of the passengers, wandering about the wreckage. I saw eight or nine people lying on the ground near the tail plane, who all appeared to be dead. In the distance I could hear Fred shouting, but I was unable to get up because of the pain in my legs.

After attending to Jennifer Curtis, Bill Howarth left her his flying gloves and then disappeared into the fog to find help. He said:

The hill was in cloud. I walked in as straight a line as possible, noting that I could find my way back to the aircraft by the occasional drops of blood I was shedding. I think I came to a fence, but in any case I saw animal tracks in the snow, which I followed.

In the swirling fog Bill Howarth made out the indistinct outline of the transmitter station building. He trudged on through the snow and arrived at the entrance. Pushing open the glass doors, he staggered in and said quite calmly: 'There has been a crash. Can you please help me?'

CHAPTER FOUR

# GHOSTS IN THE MIST

*'When we arrived at the scene the sight was appalling.'*
TV Engineer – Bob Singleton

Despite the proximity of the ITA transmitting station to the scene of the crash, none of the men working there had heard anything to alert them. The snow and dense fog had muffled all sounds of the impact. Alan Sucksmith, one of the engineers on duty that morning, gave me a first hand account of how he first heard news of the crash and his subsequent involvement in the incident.

The first thing I remember was a man coming into the entrance hall of the station with his head speckled with blood. He said there had been a crash and could we phone the police. My first reaction was, how on earth could he have got a car up there that morning through the snow, and it was a few seconds before it dawned on me that it was in fact a plane that had crashed.

Alan Sucksmith.

Bill Jarvis, the engineer in charge at the station, quickly took control of the situation and gave instructions to Alan Sucksmith to phone the police station at Horwich. PC 999 Louis Ortel – an appropriate collar number – answered the call. The phone was then handed to Detective Constable Raymond Walker Jackson and he dealt with the matter from that point on. He would later play a significant roll in the subsequent

45

investigation and reporting of the incident. That call from the snowbound transmitter station was the start of a mammoth rescue attempt ever seen in the region. Alan Sucksmith continues:

> I passed the telephone to Howarth, who gave details of the aircraft and the crash. Because of its remote location, the Winter Hill TV site was equipped with 'Z' beds and a stretcher together with the usual first aid kit. Frank Grindley said he would remain behind on site and prepare the beds to receive the injured. The remainder of the staff, carrying the stretcher and first aid kit, followed Mr Howarth – who turned out to be the First Officer – to the crash site. Bill Jarvis, the Engineer in Charge, telephoned his wife who lived on Georges Lane near our approach road, to explain what had happened and also asked her to alert our driver and handyman that the emergency services would be arriving.

> We left the station in appalling weather, low cloud down to ground level, visibility down to perhaps 20 to 30 yards, very cold and damp with varying depth of snow underfoot. We were able to retrace Mr Howarth's footprints to the crash site, which was some 400 yards or so from the station and somewhat off the track that continued over the hill to Belmont. The scene that met our eyes was one of utter carnage; the plane had broken into two major parts, the tail section, which was upright and the cockpit which was upside down. The remainder of the aircraft had broken into many parts and was scattered all around the area. It was so quiet when we got to the site. We were traumatised, but managed to stay calm. I had such an overwhelming feeling of helplessness because of the devastation.

> There were bodies with all manner of injuries lying all around, perhaps mainly within a radius of twenty to thirty yards or so. Some were crying out with a name, no doubt of their family. Our immediate priority was to help

the injured, and it didn't take much more than a glance to decide who were alive and who were dead. At this stage in my life, as a 25-year-old, I had never come across a dead body close up before, let alone in these circumstances, but, after perhaps my initial feeling of shock and helplessness, nature must have taken over and programmed us to respond in these situations, there was a job to do and we just had to get on with it.

The stewardess was still sat in her seat in the back of the plane and no doubt somewhat in shock. I think she must have been helped back to the TV station by one of my colleagues, I cannot recall helping her personally although I may have done so. Between the staff, we had a smattering of first aid knowledge but I think we all understood it could not be applied in these circumstances. It was so cold and damp and I think with some wind chill that the priority was to get the injured back to the warmth of our building; otherwise some may have died from exposure.

We found one injured man and got him onto our stretcher and started to carry him back to the station. I had never realised just how difficult it was to carry an occupied stretcher over uneven ground. It was back breaking and arm wrenching work but we managed in the end with the benefit of one or two stops. I returned to the crash again and this time came across the pilot who I later learnt was Captain Cairnes. He had injuries to his legs with bits of wire or thin tubing around them, and maybe other injuries. He was conscious and insisting that we should help all the others before we attended to him. He said: 'Don't worry about me, get the others out first.' However, we were at his side and rather than spend time looking for someone else we ignored his wishes and not without some difficulty and pain to himself got him onto the stretcher and so back to the warmth of the station.

I think by this time Mrs Jarvis, the wife of the Engineer in Charge, had arrived on site and she and Frank Grindley were looking after the injured to the best of their ability. I cannot recall carrying anyone else back to the station. I think I must have gone out to the crash again but possibly by now all the injured had been moved to our building.

A main undercarriage leg & wheel was just one of the many pieces of wreckage strewn across the hillside. *(British Pathe)*

John Hall, Shift Engineer at the station, remembers the incident somewhat differently. The following is based on his own account of the events he gave to me in 2004.

Winter Hill was my first posting working for the ITA and I had only been working there for a few months. I had been on duty for several days, staying overnight at the station because the weather was so bad. The scene outside the station on that Thursday morning was of a completely white winter's morning, terribly cold with fog, and visibility no more than thirty yards.

My car, which had brought me up to the site a couple of days previously was bogged down in the snow, some twenty yards from the station at the side of the road leading up. I had been trying to get it started when a figure appeared out of the mist – who I later learned was the co-pilot. He said there had been a crash. I realised that this explained the noise I had heard some ten minutes previously. This had sounded like a whooshing noise followed by a muffled roar in the distance, but it proved to be only about half a mile away over the hill towards Belmont.

I rushed into the station and shouted to the other engineers to come quickly to the rescue and bring the stretcher. We left Frank Grindley at the station and he raised the alarm with the emergency services. John Charlton, Bob Singleton, Alan Sucksmith and myself, along with the co-pilot, set off to the crash site, which was over the hill and in rough ground. On arrival we found the crash site completely hidden in the fog and you really couldn't see the whole area or how many people were lying injured. The body of the aircraft was smashed, but the tail section was largely intact.

Captain Cairnes was lying under the smashed cockpit section and had fractures to the lower legs. We eased him onto the stretcher by placing it near his head and pulling him onto it thereby not causing him too much pain. He was protesting that we should take someone else first, but bearing in mind the intense cold we decided not to waste valuable time. We could not see all the people on the hill, as it was very foggy at this spot. Anyway, we set off and I remember it was extremely difficult to carry the stretcher up the hill over rough and rocky ground. I remember seeing one poor man we passed who was still alive but whose head was stove in. I had never seen a dead person before this and I was in a state of shock.

We reached the station and by this time some people were arriving, having walked up from the direction of Horwich. We directed them to the crash site. Frank Grindley had meanwhile prepared some beds and we were able to put the pilot onto one of these, although I later worried that we should not have moved him off the stretcher – the stretcher was needed again.

In no time at all the station was filled with all manner of people, some from the media who were going around asking all sorts of questions. Then we had TV news people with cameras but I declined to appear, but John Charlton was interviewed. I am afraid I was too traumatised and busied myself around the transmitting station. Later I co-opted two or three people to move my car and run it down the hill to get it started – it could have been in the way of the rescue services.

Fellow engineer and rescuer, Bob Singleton also recalled his involvement:

Leaving Frank Grindley behind at the station to organise aid and man the telephone, the rest of us went out to the aircraft. The snow was two feet deep at best, much deeper in places. Visibility was about thirty yards and it was very cold. When we arrived at the scene the sight was appalling. The items we had brought were pitifully inadequate for such a situation. There were bodies all over the place. Alan Sucksmith and I walked along looking for people who were still alive. The only seats intact were in the tail section, which had broken away. Still sitting in one of them was the stewardess. She simply sat there quietly, just staring ahead.

Jennifer Curtis, cold, bleeding and shocked, describes the moment when help arrived:

After what seemed an interminable amount of time I suddenly heard voices in the distance. It was Bill Howarth with two of the engineers from the ITA station. They looked absolutely appalled. I was relieved to see them and was happy and smiling, but from the look on their faces they were absolutely shocked to see what had happened. They each put an arm around my waist to support me and helped me out of the wreckage. I was then taken to the transmitter station. What I didn't know then was that I had a dislocated left hip, which was very painful, but at the time I would have dragged anything to get away from that horrific scene.

Harold Williamson recalled:

The First Officer was very lucky when he went for help to go to the left, for he was back in twenty minutes with five men from the TV station. If he had turned right he would have travelled miles down the valley through feet of snow. The snow on top was only inches deep as the wind had blown it clear.

As the stewardess complained of being very cold and the view was very depressing, I suggested we walk to the TV station, which the engineers said was only 400 yards away. She agreed. We got out of the tail and one of the men took her by the arm and me by the hand like a child and off we went. It wasn't too bad except for crossing snowdrifts, and when my foot went down with a rush through the snow crust it didn't half touch me up. When we reached the track to the station it was better and I told the man to go ahead with the girl and I would follow at my own pace. He did this and came back for me.

It was only when Jennifer Curtis finally arrived at the transmitter station that the full extent of the disaster began to hit her. She said:

Stewardess Jennifer Curtis (Fleet) receives treatment at the station. *(Bolton Evening News)*

I saw only a few men that I knew brought in alive and I realised then that the others could not possibly have survived that crash. I remember seeing Mike Cairnes being stretchered in, he was groaning. Then soon after Norman Ennett came in – they had to bandage his head.

I was asked if I would like to contact anybody. I said yes, I would like to phone my father, because I thought this is something big and it's going to be on the television and on the radio. I didn't want him to hear the news and wonder what had happened to me. I remember ringing my father and saying to him: 'Dad. We've crashed.' Dad was very philosophical and never liked to think any thing bad, so he said: 'No, what you actually mean Jennifer is that you've landed.' I said: 'No I don't. We've actually crashed.' He said: 'Alright, where are you?' I said: 'I think it's an ITV station.' He said: 'Just stay there and people will come and help you.' I said:

'Oh yes, they are. I just wanted to let you know that we had crashed and I don't want you to worry if you see it on the television or hear it on the radio.'

The telephone I was using was a big old-fashioned type with a cupped mouthpiece. What I didn't realise at the time was that I had a broken nose and a fracture of the upper jaw and all the time I was talking to my father, blood was continually pouring out into the mouthpiece. Fortunately, the man in whose office I was calling from must have been a very heavy smoker and had a big glass ashtray into which I kept emptying the blood.

Dad, who knew the crew, asked how Mike Cairnes was. I told him he had just been brought in and that Bill Howarth was able to walk around and that he had got help for us. After speaking to my father I felt much better. I thought, that's it, everything is now going to be OK, and I don't need to worry. People will come and help.

At that stage, Mrs Jarvis, the station manager's wife arrived at the station and because I was the only female she was asked to look after me. She made me a cup of hot tea and piled me with blankets. Sometime later the ambulance people came and I remember Bill Howarth watching me being bandaged up. Then newspaper reporters arrived and began taking my photograph. Bill didn't like that; I think it agitated him a bit.

I can't remember the duration of time from being taken to the station to when the ambulance came. I do remember I was the last to be taken down as I had fewer injuries compared to the others. I remember I wanted to walk to the ambulance but they said no I would have to go on a stretcher. As I was being taken out there were policemen looking at me and press photographers taking photographs of me as well.

First Officer Bill Howarth at the transmitter station.
*(Bolton Evening News)*

Harold Williamson recalls his arrival at the station:

We got inside and sat down in a palatial hall for the situation. They had four beds laid out and hot tea ready. The sweat was pouring off me but my feet were like ice – they didn't get hot until the middle of the night. The stewardess then rang her father up at Arbory Vicarage and I rang Mr Douglass (the engineer at the Isle of Man Electricity Board) at the office, as I knew my wife Margaret was out. The Chief Engineer's wife then arrived, having walked up two miles from her house, and washed our faces and gave us more tea. She gave me the *Daily Telegraph* to read and left me in her husband's office. I was very nearly forgotten in there when they started carting us away. I was in the last ambulance with the stewardess but had to be carried out as I had stiffened up. The ride down the mountain was hell; the frozen bumps gave my ribs a proper shaking.

Norman Ennett, who remained sheltering in the shattered remains of the cockpit talking to Mike Cairnes whilst waiting for help to arrive, passed the time in a fruitless search for his missing shoe and wristwatch. He said:

> About half an hour passed when I heard the muffled voices of people approaching in the mist, it was Bill Howarth returning with three or four fellows from the TV station. I climbed out through the gaping hole in the side of the cockpit to meet them. One of the engineers gave me his duffle coat to wear as it was sleeting heavily and I was very cold. They then helped me to walk over to the station where I was given a very welcome cup of hot tea. Soon after the other survivors began to come in. Eventually a doctor and some police officers managed to get up the hill on foot. I was immediately given a shot of morphine to help the pain and sometime later an ambulance took me to the Bolton Royal Infirmary.

Survivor Fred Kennish, suffering multiple injuries, was at first left for dead in the gasping cold on the hillside. He explained to me what happened:

> All I know after the crash is what Bill Jarvis told me many years later – he was the Chief Engineer at the station and I believe one of the first on the scene. He said he found me in a snowdrift, and then he heard others calling for help and thought they had a better chance of survival. He straightened my leg, which was lying across my chest and put me into a dying position! He said it was an awful decision to have to make. Luckily two firemen found me later, one of them strapped me to a ladder with his tunic belt and they carried me off the moor. Sometime later in the ambulance I must have regained consciousness, I remember gulping for air and the air

seemed to going straight through a hole in my back – it just felt as if I was dying.

Local reporters were some of the first to make their way to the scene and on arrival found themselves at the very heart of the rescue efforts. One of the journalists gave the following account:

We were given a shovel apiece and we hurried up the road to the ITA station, overtaking ambulance men and firemen struggling through the snow with stretchers, blankets and sacks of dressings

Parties of men from Montcliffe Quarry and Bottom o' th' Moor were furiously digging to clear the drifts. The road was blocked in over a dozen places, and some of the drifts were many feet deep. Soon after Georges Lane we met a fire engine backing down, unable to get any further.

At the transmitter station rescue operations were badly hindered by the lack of stretchers. My first job was to carry a can of petrol to a spot on the road where they hoped a helicopter would land. As soon as two other reporters arrived with a stretcher I went with them towards the wreckage. Visibility was only a few yards, and although footprints and bloodstains in the snow marked the way, we lost our bearings after 200 yards.

Then we met a stretcher party carrying the last injured passenger back to the station. They were a man short so I joined them. The passenger was unconscious and in a pretty bad way. I saw one passenger reach the transmitter station on foot, guided by an ambulance man. He was wearing a raincoat and still carrying a travelling bag in his hand. We cut arrows in the snow to guide other rescuers.

Another reporter wrote:

The scene at the crash was almost beyond description. The main part of the fuselage was upside down in a splintered heap, and bodies were everywhere in the drifts of snow. One was trapped beneath an engine, which was lying with its propellers buckled and twisted. Nearby one of the wheels was buried in the ground. The tail section was lying 50 yards away quite upright, the seats in the rear still intact and a telephone was still on its hook. The toilet at the very back was completely undamaged. Personal belongings were scattered everywhere, mingled with yellow life jackets. One of the dead was still clutching a paper he was reading.

PC John Atkinson, based at Horwich police station, who was one of the first police officers to reach the scene said:

At 10:00 am on Thursday, 27 February, I was off duty when I received a telephone call from Sergeant Bradbury, informing me that an aeroplane had crashed on Winter Hill. I put on my uniform and went to Horwich Police Station and reported to Inspector Lloyd. I then set out for Montcliffe, arriving there at 10:30. I saw that large snowdrifts blocked the access road to the transmitter station. At the time it was sleeting hard and the visibility was very poor.

After obtaining permission from Sergeant Bradbury, I asked for two ambulance men to volunteer to accompany me on foot to the scene with first-aid kits. With an ambulance man called Diggins and a fireman we set off to make our way to the crash site, cutting across fields to avoid the deep drifts. Another ambulance man followed behind with blankets.

We eventually arrived at the transmitter station at 10:55 and saw two of the station engineers carrying an empty stretcher from the front entrance. They informed me that several survivors were already inside and required first-aid. I instructed Diggins to go in and give them assistance. I then accompanied the two engineers to the crash scene. On the way we met First Officer Howarth, he was covered in blood, but he said that he was all right and could walk. A little further on we met Mr Jarvis and a stretcher party carrying a survivor, the fireman accompanied them back to the station and Mr Jarvis guided us to the crash site to point out where the two remaining casualties were. It was now raining hard and the visibility was still poor. I met sub officer Lee and his men carrying a survivor on a ladder towards the station.

On my arrival at the scene I saw that bodies were scattered in a wide circle around the wreckage, a large number on the port side of the tail plane, the two remaining survivors were about twenty yards away. They had been covered in coats from the dead for warmth. The ambulance man carrying blankets then joined us, we wrapped them around the casualties and placed one of them on the stretcher and the engineers took him back to the station.

I then made a search of the bodies to see if I could find any that were alive, but was unable to do so. I noticed the aircraft had broken into two parts. The wreckage of the wings and the cockpit were about fifty yards from the tail, which was intact to just in front of the entrance door. I entered this section and searched it for further casualties. On the deck near the door I found the logbook and copies of the passenger manifest. I then made my way to the transmitter station. On the way I directed a stretcher party to the other injured man. In the distance I could hear some men shouting, but because of the visibility I was unable to see them. I shouted directions to them, that, when they found the wreckage to make a search for any survivors.

On my arrival at the station, the ambulance men and

engineers were treating the injured. I checked the names of the survivors who were conscious with the passenger list. From the stewardess I ascertained the exact number of passengers and crew on board the aircraft. The time was now 11:30, so I took control of the telephone and set up an incident post. I spoke to Sergeant Bradbury at the Montcliffe incident post below and updated him on the situation. I then spoke to Horwich Police Station and made an urgent request for further first-aid equipment and assistance to be sent to the scene.

By 11:40 all the survivors had been brought into the station. About this time Chief Superintendent Spencer, Chief Inspector Twiddy, Detective Inspector Naylor and DC Vernon arrived. I informed them of the situation and what I had done. I was instructed to control the incident post, where I remained until 5:40 pm when all the bodies had been removed.

As ambulances and fire appliances stood by at Horwich, three RAF helicopters were scrambled from Valley in Anglesey and Leconfield in Yorkshire. The plan was for a doctor in the first helicopter to land at the scene and assess the situation and request further help if necessary. They arrived over Horwich late in the morning. A signal fire was lit at the junction of Victoria Road and Church Street, but because of the bad visibility it was not seen and made their use in the rescue operation impossible. Finally one of the helicopters landed on spare land on the Hilton Estate where it remained on standby until the late afternoon. Also alerted were the mountain rescue team based at Harper Hill, Buxton, but by the time they arrived by road shortly after 2 pm they found the main rescue work had taken place.

Winnie Jarvis, wife of the Engineer in Charge at the station, heard the news of the crash when the telephone rang in their bungalow on Georges Lane at the bottom of Winter Hill. She said:

I was busy cleaning when the telephone rang and my husband told me the devastating news that there had been an aircrash on Winter Hill. He told me to go and find Mr Peacock, the driver, and tell him to get up there as quickly as possible. I went up to the corner of the lane to find him digging out the snow around the Land Rover. Whilst I was telling him the news, a fire engine turned into the lane and pulled up. They could go no further because of the snow, which was about four or five feet deep. I told them they would have to walk up and if they didn't know the way I would show them.

They got axes and other bits of equipment from their appliance and we all set off together. It normally takes about half an hour to walk up to the station, but it took us a lot longer because the snow was so deep. The mist was dreadful that morning; you could just about see your hand in front of you. We walked on and on and eventually came to the Scotsman's Post, which is directly opposite the station.

When we entered the building the stewardess and a passenger had already been rescued. The stewardess had lost her shoes and was in a very dazed state, as was the man. Then they brought in two other men who were badly injured including the pilot. The engineers were short of a stretcher, so they took a ladder and went back out and found another survivor and brought him back to the station. I took hold of his hand; he was in a very bad way.

At that time there were very few people to do anything; there was only the engineers and my husband. I was fully occupied, making tea and seeing first to one and then another as the survivors were brought in. I tried to calm them down, as they were all very dazed and shocked.

Sometime later a local doctor and a nurse arrived; they had managed to walk up. Later I went with them to the crash scene – it was a dreadful sight to behold.

Ambulance driver, Cliff Smalley, based at the King Street Ambulance Station, Farnworth, recalls being called out that morning:

An Ambulance finally makes it to the fog bound transmitter station. *(British Pathe)*

A call came through that an aeroplane had crashed on Winter Hill. At the time I was driving a twelve-seater Commer ambulance, with an attendant, Cliff Haskins. We proceeded to the scene through Bolton and along Chorley Old Road. It had been snowing and was very foggy. The roads were fairly clear – the amount of traffic was not like it is today.

We arrived at the bottom of Georges Lane and could see that the snow was two foot deep at least. I decided to put on snow chains, which we all carried then. My attendant, Cliff, set out on foot to the scene – which turned out to be a two mile trek – carrying a collapsible stretcher and blankets. I carried on up a dirt track, which leads to the TV station and parked up at a farmhouse. Eventually a snowplough and salt wagon arrived and managed to clear the road. Meanwhile an ambulance officer had arrived and we drove up as far as the station. The track was very narrow with only space for one vehicle at a time. All operations were co-ordinated from my vehicle radio by the officer – radio contact then was new and had only recently been installed. At the time the wreckage could not be seen from where we were because of the fog. Later, when the mist started to lift I could see the plane debris. The front section was all over the place, but about one third of the fuselage containing the tail was all in one piece. People were all around recovering the bodies and collecting belongings from the wreckage.

The survivors found were taken to the TV station and given treatment. After a while the First Officer was brought to my vehicle and was able to sit up all the way to Bolton Royal Infirmary. After this my part in the operation was finished and I returned to Farnworth Station. I have no idea how long all this took, as time seemed immaterial.

Meanwhile, another attempt to reach the scene was being made from the village of Belmont on the northern side of Winter Hill. Belmont was only a mile from the crash site, but the footpath to the summit was almost obliterated by snow and judged unsuitable for large-scale rescue operations. Nevertheless, a rescue party of Bolton Borough Police officers made preparations for an attempt.

Jack Kay, the postmaster in Belmont village, remembers that rescue party and how he first heard news of the disaster:

Most of us knew nothing about it. I remember my wife being out at the back of the shop during the morning and hearing a bang, but at the time it didn't seem anything unusual, it could well have been the sound of the gamekeepers' shotgun up on the moors above the township.

It was only later, when his post office was invaded by a stream of police officers and rescuers that he realised something was seriously wrong. But still, there were no hints as to the enormity of the tragedy. Jack continues:

> I remember them crowding into my shop, they wanted chocolate, and plenty of it – obviously to keep them going in the cold on the hillside. I asked them what all the fuss was about, but they seemed as much in the dark as we were. All they knew was that they were on their way to some accident. Although they were less than a mile from the scene they still didn't seem to know what was up. It was a complete mystery. There was no fire on the hillside; you would expect a plane to go up in flames. But there was nothing.

As the rescue party set off in the slanting snow from Belmont village to battle their way over the desolate moorland in an attempt to reach the disaster scene, gamekeeper Charles Hutchings was doing his rounds of the estate, which was administered then by Bolton Waterworks. Earlier that morning he had set off at his normal time, following the paths over the moor he had walked for more than 30 years. At some point the Wayfarer must have flown above him, but because of the thick layer of snow and dense fog he had heard and seen nothing. He was on his way home to his lodge for lunch, when he spotted the Belmont rescue party weaving their way up the hillside, like ghosts in the mist.

> I went over to ask what they were doing and it was only then that I found out what had happened. Although I had been out on the estate all morning, I had heard and seen nothing. I joined the party and we set off towards the summit. We wandered in and out of the mist and ended up miles off course. No one knew where they were going and we must have walked around in circles. If no one had reached the crash from the access road God knows how long it might have taken us to reach the wreck.

We eventually reached the crash site an hour and a half after the aircraft came down. Although all the bodies had been taken away by then, it was still enough to shock me deeply. There were twenty to thirty people standing around the wreckage looking dazed, I think they must have been the rescuers. They looked shocked enough to be survivors themselves.

Starboard side of the tail section showing the extensive damage. *(Bolton Evening News)*

Clifford Greenhalgh, who lived in the Sharples district of Bolton at the time, first heard news of the crash on the radio. Without hesitation he donned his coat and set off from his home in an attempt to make his way to the scene to render what assistance he could. Speaking on the summit of Winter Hill on the 43rd anniversary of the disaster in 2001, he said:

> Things I did on the day are now a bit vague, although certain parts are still imprinted on my mind. Soon after hearing news of the crash I left my home in Athlone Avenue and walked past Smithills Hall onto Smithills Dean Road. Whilst on the road, a Land Rover pulled up

and the driver said he was attempting to get to the crash site and could I direct him. We travelled together onto Scouts Road and stopped at a farmhouse opposite the path that led up to Winter Hill. After enquiries at the farm we were told that it was impossible to reach our destination because the snow had obliterated any signs of the path. The only other way was up Georges Lane, assuming that it too had not been blocked.

When we arrived at the access road to Winter Hill we were told we would have quite a job to get up because of the snowdrifts. We left the Land Rover there and struggled our way up on foot. When we finally arrived at the scene it was very misty. The first thing we saw was the tail section of the plane and standing nearby was a police officer. On the ground at his feet was what I took to be a blanket filled with the personal belongings of the victims. He asked us what we were doing and we told him we had come to help in whatever way we could. He said: 'It's too late to help these poor devils.'

The Land Rover driver was detailed to search for body parts and anything else, and mark them with white sticks. I was taken to a row of bodies laid out on the ground. Told to tie their arms across their chests, straighten their legs and tie them together with scarves, whilst they still could be moved, as they had been there some time and it was getting colder all the time.

Whilst I was carrying out this task, I could not help but shed a few tears at the thought that only a brief few hours ago these men and boys had been laughing and joking with one another. The state of the bodies was a terrible sight to witness. The police officer came over to see how I was getting on and asked me if I felt all right. I told him I was as right as I could be under the circumstances.

I lost all count of time. Cold and wet through, we

began putting the bodies into ambulances, and then we too were taken down to the bottom of the hill. There we were directed to a mobile canteen and told to drink as much hot soup as we needed. It was then the reaction set in. Suddenly I was violently sick and began to tremble from head to toe.

As I said, things are now very vague, and now at the age of seventy-three my memory is not as vivid as it used to be. But I shall always have permanently etched in my mind the first sights of the tragedy. The police officer standing beside the wrecked tail section; the personal belongings of the victims laid out on the blanket; the row of bodies; and not to be forgotten, that of a woman spectator allowing her dog off the lead to run among the dead and who remonstrated with me for kicking the dog away.

Another local man involved in the rescue was John Sanderson, licensee of the Jolly Crofters public house, situated at the bottom of Winter Hill. Although John died in April 2003, his daughter, Barbara Cursley gave me the following account of his involvement taken from her father's memoirs. He wrote:

A major incident that occurred during my time at the Jolly Crofters was the tragic air disaster that happened on Winter Hill one Thursday morning in February 1958. The area between Horwich and Bolton was snowbound and all the roads impassable and shrouded in mist. The First Officer from the plane, miraculously locating the Winter Hill Transmitting Station, raised the alarm. The Chief Engineer, Bill Jarvis alerted the emergency services – then all hell broke loose.

John Sanderson. *(Barbara Cursley)*

The company operating Montcliffe Quarry had put all available resources to clear the length of Georges Lane between its workings and the main road, which was finished on Wednesday late afternoon. On this Thursday morning, Jack Speight was delivering orders at Montcliffe when Mrs Jarvis gave him the news of the disaster and urged him to recruit as many people as possible to form a digging party to clear the snow blocking the initial length – about half a mile – of the road from Georges Lane to the TV station.

After Jack had alerted the men from the quarry, who left work on the road to start the necessary dig, he called for me and with John Shawcross we drove up the hill to join the digging party. As we were labouring, somewhat frantically, I remember members of the medical and emergency services were making the long trek to the scene of the disaster manhandling stretchers, blankets etc.

We concentrated on digging through a long deep gully, all the while wondering as to the extent of the disaster. As we were nearing the end of the gully a police officer told us a snow-moving machine had been requested from RAF Weeton, near Preston. This duly arrived, and after a spluttering start went on its way to clear the length of the road to the TV station. We were relieved of our task and advised to go home for a well-earned rest and refreshment. There were people and vehicles in plenty on Georges Lane and Montcliffe. The police allowed only emergency services personnel to enter the road to the station. All three of us left in Jack's van for home. On coming in sight of the Jolly Crofters it was to behold a chaotic scene of vehicles, prominent being the BBC Outside Broadcast Unit. The pub would become the centre for communication and thrust me in deep involvement.

I anticipated there being plenty of people inside and decided to go in by the back door and have a change of clothes before going into the bar. I had no sooner entered the dining room than was confronted by the redoubtable BBC presenter, Alan Dixson with his recorder. He had fixed it with my wife, Ruth, to get to me before the press reporters. A lengthy question and answer interview was conducted and dispatched post haste to Manchester for the main hourly news item. I went into the pub bar to find Ruth and volunteer helpers doing their utmost to cope with the demands of the horde of media reporters. I was trying to help but was hindered by constant questioning from the reporters. They were not allowed to visit the scene, but to read reports in the newspapers the following day one would have thought they had.

A further request came from the Outside BBC Unit headed by celebrated commentator, Kenneth Wolstenholme, to use one of the public rooms to be able to transmit news of the disaster for the six o'clock TV news. The transmitting van was parked outside the window, cables passing through to camera equipment. He arranged for Jack Speight and me to be interviewed, giving a summary of our part in the disaster. I have a photograph taken from the TV by Jack's father-in-law recording the interview.

Jack Speight & John Sanderson being interviewed by Kenneth Wolstenholme for the BBC News. *(Barbara Cursley)*

For several days there was interest in the disaster, the site and wrecked aircraft were closely guarded until eventual removal. We had a request from the police to accommodate an inspector from the Civil Aviation Authority. His visit was to see the site and record the damage to the plane. On the following Sunday afternoon he took Ruth and me to the site, being the first laypeople allowed. The inspector released the plane for removal, which was done by a group of aircraft technicians from Speke, Liverpool. All bits and pieces had to be salvaged for reconstruction. During the time of this operation the men came for lunch and called in the evening on their way home. To my surprise and delight a piece of the air craft mounted and suitably inscribed arrived by post a few months later with a note of appreciation. The plaque was placed on a pillar in the entrance hall of the Jolly Crofters.

The final chapter in my involvement in the sequence of events of the disaster was the Inquest. This was convened in the Mechanics Institute, Horwich. The Coroner at the time was Mr R. M. Barlow, a solicitor in practice in Bury. He was a stern, sharp character who dispensed his official capacity with pomp severity. A jury was formed of licensees and pensioners assembled by a local police officer, Jack Atkinson, who had been appointed Coroner's Officer. The proceedings lasted three days during which time evidence given by numerous witnesses was called and cross-examination by the legal profession very much under the watchful eye of the Coroner. It was a relief when the verdict of misadventure was announced and the Inquest closed.

It was an amusing sight to see the Coroner making little piles of coins so carefully and scrooge-like for the meagre payment to each Jury member for expenses. He generously absolved all Jury members from further Jury service for life.

The disaster had the effect of bringing together in friendship the Rotary Club of Horwich – of which I was a member – and the Rotary Club of Douglas. Members made exchange visits, and the Douglas Club donated a seat which they brought over from the Isle of Man, and it was placed in the small park at the corner of Lever Park, in a position from which Winter Hill can be seen.

John Sanderson's daughter, Barbara Cursley, was a schoolgirl at the time and shares similar memories. She said:

For three days we were snowed in and on the fourth day the road was clear enough to be able to walk to the grammar school in Rivington with the other children from our side of Horwich. I remember being in the Chemistry Lab and a message coming through to tell us of the Winter Hill air disaster. Also that one of the local farmers would be coming down on his tractor to pick us up from school. As we were passing Victoria Methodist church on our way home we saw stretchers going in, later to be told the church was being used as a morgue.

When I arrived home at the Jolly Crofters the car park in front of the pub was full, predominant was one of the BBC Outside Broadcasting vans – television then was in its infancy – where I was able to watch the interview of Jack Speight and my father. Chemistry homework loomed, however, the journalists filing their copy using our telephone distracted me and I listened wide-eyed with wonderment at the way they were able to embellish the story and a little disgusted at taking journalistic licence.

Keith Raynerd was a 19-year-old police constable and had just recently been posted to Farnworth Police Station. He told fellow researcher, Paul Lomax of his involvement:

On that day I paraded for duty at 6:00 am at Farnworth Police Station, together with Jack Wilkinson with whom I shared digs. Our shift should have been from 6 till 2. The day was awful, raining, sleeting etc. For some reason we were allowed to go to our digs for breakfast – I think Jack went before me and I went about 10 am. Whilst I was having my breakfast the area car called round and I was told that there had been an air crash on Winter Hill in the Horwich sector.

As many officers that could be spared were immediately taken up to the scene from their various stations in the Division – these included Jack and myself. When we arrived at Winter Hill we were told of the extent of the crash, that there were survivors, but over thirty people were probably dead. Their bodies were spread over the moorland surrounding the crash scene. The officer in charge was I believe Chief Inspector Sydney Twiddy, the Divisional second-in-command.

Police Officers Keith Raynerd & Jack Wilkinson - wearing capes - stretcher a victim off the moor. *(Manchester Evening News)*

Together with other services a sweep search was organised. The weather was atrocious. It was intermittently sleeting and raining. Underfoot it was muddy and swampy and we sank a good few inches as we walked along. As the sweep progressed, bodies, and parts of bodies were found and taken back to a central point. I can't remember how long the search carried on for, but when it was finished all the bodies were checked and when all the passengers and crew were accounted for we were given a meal, which had been arranged locally. Eventually we were stood down – this must have been late in the afternoon.

Later the following week I was on night duty and was detailed to spend the night on Winter Hill as the wreckage had to be guarded. This was because members of the public had been taking souvenirs from the plane.

Luckily, nothing happened during the night I was there with another officer.

I was only 19 years of age. I'd never seen a violent death before this – I saw many after – and obviously it made a lasting impression on me. Nowadays people would have counselling, but in those days it was hardly heard of. By going for a drink in the evening afterwards, Jack and I were able to talk everything through and helped each other to come to terms with what had happened.

Station Engineer, Alan Sucksmith, said of the aftermath:

Perhaps getting on for some two hours after the crash, the official rescue services began to arrive and our role became one of extending to them the various facilities of the TV station and answering the many telephone calls that were coming in – some from the relatives on the Isle of Man. I think the Fire Service staff were the first ones to walk up the hill to the site together with a local doctor. I believe it was later in the morning when the vehicles began to arrive, the snow having been cleared from the approach road by the efforts of the men from the local quarry and the coalmine, together with the RAF Sno-Cat, which had been diverted from clearing snow on the Blackrod by-pass.

The rescue services removed the dead from the scene and placed them in our garage before removing them to more suitable premises in Horwich. I have always thought that the people who undertook this task must have had a much more traumatic experience than myself and colleagues who were only concerned with getting the injured to a safe place and looking after them as well as we could.

Mrs Jarvis, the wife of our Engineer in Charge, was to be congratulated. Although in her fifties, as soon as her husband told her that there had been a plane crash, she walked up the hill, through the snow, and once on the site did what she could to provide help and comfort to the survivors.

I cannot recall any details from late morning onwards. I presume that once the rescue services had arrived, they must have taken charge and with increased manpower available to them our direct assistance was no longer required in the aftermath of the crash. To some extent, and as far as was possible in the circumstances, we must have resumed our normal duties for the afternoon. Later on, together with other staff, I was interviewed briefly on the ITN News around six o'clock.

The staff that were involved with the rescue operations were told not to report for work for the next few days and when we did return much activity around the crash site and TV station was concerned with establishing the cause of the crash and clearing up the wreckage. There were many visitors, both official and unofficial, to the site over the next days and weeks.

Reporter, Peter Elkinskas, had just returned from reporting from the snowbound Woodhead Pass, when on hearing news of the crash immediately set off for Winter Hill. Here is his dramatic report, which appeared in the *Daily Mail* the following day and which gives the reader some idea of the terrible conditions all the rescuers faced to reach the scene.

I took my skis to Winter Hill yesterday to reach the scene of the airliner disaster. But this time they were no use to me. The snow was too slushy. So I set off up the hill in my ski boots.

The scramble up the 1,450 feet hill took me 50

minutes. I sampled the difficulties the rescue teams had already beaten in their race to the crash.

Twice I floundered up to my waist in snowdrifts. Several times I waded knee deep in slush, as they had to do. More than once I lost my way in the mist and drizzle that cut visibility to a few yards.

The smell of scorched rubber on the wind was my guide as it was for the rescue teams. At last I heard voices, then saw ghostly shadows moving through the mist. On the left, the tail loomed. Before me was a tangled mass of wreckage in which the rescuers were at work.

When I arrived all the living had been brought out and were being treated in the ITA transmitting station 400 yards away. A bulldozer was shoving snow off the track that leads to the station. Behind it was a stream of ambulances.

The efficiency of the rescue organisation impressed me. Quietly, apparently unhurried, the police, firemen, and the ambulance crews had not wasted a second.

Captain Mike Cairnes, lying badly injured on a camp bed in the transmitter station recalled the moment when the first of the rescuers and doctors arrived:

There were six or seven of us in this room at the TV station waiting for help to arrive. Eventually a doctor somehow got to us and pointing at me, said: 'I want him to go first.' I insisted that the passengers should go first. He said: 'Shut up. You're not in command up here, I am. You are to go first.'

So anyhow, they took me on a stretcher to the ambulance – one of the old Austin Princess 4 litre jobs, a big heavy two-ton monster. As we went bumping down the hill towards Bolton I refused to lie down and sat up still holding my foot against my chest. The aged nurse, who was about seventy said: 'Please lie down.' I said: 'No thanks, I like to see where I'm going.'

It was snowing like billy-o when we came into Bolton and as far as the eye could see the traffic lights were on green. From where I was seated I could just see the speedometer needle flickering on seventy. Jesus Christ, I thought if one of those lights suddenly changes to red … I've just survived an air crash and then I'm spent in an ambulance crash!

# CHAPTER FIVE

# THE AFTERMATH

*'It was all so tragic. We did what we could.'*
Sheila Ashton

Despite the super-human efforts of all those involved in the rescue, the final cold statistics told their own story. Of the 42 passengers and crew on board Charlie Sierra only nine emerged from the devastation – injured, but alive. One passenger subsequently died of his injuries at the ITA transmitter station. The rest, with varying degrees of injury were taken to Bolton Royal Infirmary. It was the close proximity of the TV station that probably saved the lives of those few survivors. If Bill Howarth had not been able to stagger the 400 yards to raise the alarm, the wreckage might not have been found in the fog and snowbound conditions for many hours.

From the moment the telephone rang in the accident room giving the news of the disaster, Bolton Royal Infirmary staff had everything under control. Immediately a major accident plan was initiated for the first time since it was put together after the Harrow rail disaster in 1952.

Joan Halliwell, a 20-year-old newly qualified radiographer, was on duty at the Infirmary on the morning of the crash. She said:

I shall never forget the day of the accident. At about ten o'clock that morning I x-rayed a lady from the Royal Ordinance Factory at Euxton who had had her fingers blown off whilst packing a detonator, she was in a dreadful mess. Then, at coffee time we heard the news on the radio about the air crash on Winter Hill.

Immediately the hospital was cleared of all outpatients and non-urgent cases. Casualty was transformed with bench beds and all sorts of equipment ready for a major accident. All the doctors scrubbed up ready and even the dentist donned a green gown and white Wellingtons. We had no idea how many patients would arrive, and because of the snow and fog, when they would arrive. We sat around just waiting. Then, I think it was about two o'clock, the first of the casualties started to arrive.

Also on duty was third-year Student Nurse Marion Jane. Forty years on she recalls her involvement.

I was on duty in Patrick Ward that morning, which was a male surgical and orthopaedic ward. I was giving one of the patients, called Charlie, a saline bath, when the Ward Sister came in to tell me that there had been a plane crash, and that Patrick Ward had been designated to receive survivors. At that time we did not have any details regarding the number of survivors. The usual procedure regarding the reception of accident victims was for them to be received through the Casualty Department. But on this occasion it was decided to admit any survivors directly to the wards.

Shortly after news of the crash reached us, we were told to expect a lot of survivors. Medical staff, including Consultants, arrived on the ward and it was decided that all the beds must be vacated to make way for the injured. The doctors then assessed all the current patients on the ward. Some were discharged home and those who couldn't be discharged were temporarily housed in the Physiotherapy Department so that their beds could be freed up in the event they would be needed. Our off-duty was cancelled and I think other staff may have been drafted in or put on standby. I was instructed to remain on duty and we all worked very hard to get all the beds and lockers cleaned and prepared. Trolleys for setting up infusions and transfusions were made ready, together with other emergency treatments such as tracheotomy and chest drainage, oxygen equipment etc. It must be remembered that we did not have any of the medical technology available today, such as ventilators and monitors, at our disposal.

In the meantime various reports were coming in regarding the number of survivors. I can remember feeling very elated when we were told to expect a lot. When later it was confirmed that there were only a few, I felt terrible.

After what seemed an age, the first casualty, Mr Partington, arrived on the ward. He was still conscious though profoundly shocked. I was designated to 'special' him, which meant that I was to stay by his bedside, carry out all the observations required and assist the medical staff with his treatment and care. Sadly, Mr Partington lapsed into unconsciousness and died that evening. Eventually, after all the survivors had been admitted and treated, the patients who were waiting in the Physiotherapy Department were returned to Patrick Ward as we attempted to get things back to normal. I can't remember what time I got off duty on that day, only that I was very tired. The survivors who weren't treated on Patrick Ward went to Barnes Ward, the stewardess to Nicholson Ward. All went on to make a good recovery.

Sometime after the accident and when the survivors had been discharged from our care, the Matron, Miss Moore sent for me. She told me a week's holiday was being offered to two of the nursing staff that had been involved with caring for the accident victims. She had decided that one should go from Patrick and one from

Barnes. I felt very honoured to be offered one of the places, and along with the Junior Sister from Barnes Ward, Margaret Thomasson, spent a VIP week on the Isle of Man. The Airline flew us over – I was petrified – and we stayed in the Palace View Hotel, courtesy of the owners. We were taken around the island by a taxi firm, whom I think had had a relative on the fatal flight, and I can recall having a free night out at the Villa-Marina where Ivy Benson's band was playing. We also met the Mayor and signed the visitors' book. Everyone on the island made us very welcome.

After his somewhat hair raising dash through the streets of Bolton, Captain Mike Cairnes arrived at the Infirmary without further mishap. He was stretchered from the ambulance by waiting porters, his hands raised to his bandaged head. A label tied to his coat informed the medical staff what treatment he had been given on the way. Mike Cairnes told me:

On arrival at the infirmary they put me on a trolley and dashed through the hospital. There were two surgeons, one on each side of me reducing my fractures as we went along. I looked to my starboard and there was this little nurse, she had no bra on, you could literally see everything! Now, I'm not that sort of person you understand, but for some reason I leaned over and bit her just above the nipple. She screamed – not unnaturally – I was of course suffering from shock. One of the surgeons shouted at her:

'What's the matter girl?'
'He's bitten me.' She said indignantly.
'Don't disturb the poor man.' The surgeon snapped back.

Sometime later she came and showed me the scar and I gave her a box of Black Magic chocolates – so I think I was forgiven for that unfortunate incident.

Later that evening I was moved up to a ward. At the end of the row of beds they were dealing with a man, then he was taken away and we were all moved up. Then the next man was moved up. Good God I thought, they're dead. I'm next!

The Ward Sister eventually went off duty to have her supper and on looking around I noticed what we called 'little green stripes' – nurse trainees - about on the ward. I said to one:

'Look, I'm hungry.'
'You can't eat Captain Cairnes,' she said, 'you've got very serious internal injuries.'
'Well, I can't feel them, and anyway, when I don't feel well and feel weak I like to eat.'

Somehow I eventually managed to persuade her, and soon after she brought me a boiled egg and a cup of tea. I threw up the first one but eventually got it all down. The next morning the surgeon and all his entourage behind him breezed through the ward and stopped by my bed. 'Ah Captain Cairnes,' he said, 'I think that you might have a little sustenance today.' I thought to myself, it's all right mate, I've already had it! From that point on I never looked back in my recovery.

Also lying in the Infirmary receiving treatment was Norman Ennett. He told me:

In the crash I had broken my forearm, shoulder and wrist, all on the left side. The Perspex splinter was removed from above my right eye, my head was shaved and a lot of stitches put in. My wife flew over the same evening to see me. She came into the ward and walked right past me. Had she forgotten what I looked like? I shouted to her. On turning round and seeing me she burst into tears.

It wasn't until I got out of bed the next day or so and went to the toilet. I looked in the mirror, then looked to see who was standing by me, as I didn't even recognise myself. My head was twice its normal size and the whites of my eyes were blood red.

I was flown home a week later by Manx Airlines from Blackpool and spent the next three months in plaster before being fit enough to return to work.

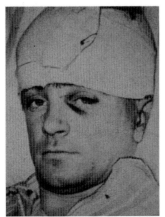

Survivor Norman Ennett in Bolton Royal
Infirmary the day after the crash. *(Bolton Evening News)*

In a letter to a relative, written with some humour from his hospital bed, survivor Harold Williamson described his time at the Infirmary:

At the hospital the whole of Bolton seemed to be on duty. I was whipped, needles jabbed into me, undressed, examined, legs, pelvis and chest x-rayed and put to bed. I was just left lying there as they didn't know if I had to go to the theatre or not, so I was not allowed any food or drink. I was left to the last as being the least damaged. About 10 pm they decided to leave me until morning, so I was given a cup of tea. I was as hungry as the devil but they wouldn't give me any food. I was filled with dope and left to sleep which I did partly. Next morning I didn't want any breakfast, I was examined again, neck x-rayed and left. That day wasn't too bad, I couldn't move but was not uncomfortable and had lots of visitors, and Margaret arrived in the evening. I was doped again at night and slept for two hours and awakened in hell. I was just beginning to get my feel back and everything was agony. They eventually gave me another jab and I slept till morning.

On Saturday morning I was washed, cleaned and had my chest x-rayed again. The final verdict is – one cracked shinbone, three cracked vertebrae and two cracked ribs. I have not been bandaged, as they believe in movement. I have to do deep breathing, which is a bit dicey, waggle my legs and toes – which is easy – and try to turn over, which, up to this morning was impossible, but I can now do it both ways, slow motion of course.

I am feeling fine now and in a day or two they will strap my shin and ankle and I will have to walk. When I can walk I can go home. I am eating like a horse and my corner of the ward is like a Harvest Home. I have had fruit and flowers from every traveller in Lancashire, books from London and I don't know what. I am thinking of setting up a stall now I am getting mobile and flogging the lot!

I have just had dinner and now have to get back into bed, been up one and a half hours. Send this letter to Jim, it will save me writing to him, I have dozens to write – could do with a blonde secretary!

\*\*\*\*\*\*\*\*\*\*\*\*\*\*\*\*\*\*\*\*\*\*\*\*\*\*\*\*\*\*\*

It was obvious from the outset that few could have survived the terrible carnage of the crash. In the late afternoon as the dusk intensified the gloom, the casualties were brought down from the hillside by relays of ambulances, an taken to the Victoria Road Methodist Church in Horwich, which was put to use as a temporary mortuary. Silent knots of spectators stood by in the darkness as the victims, shrouded in red blankets, were carried on stretchers into the church. Shortly before six o'clock the last victim was brought in and the doors were shut from prying eyes.

Each body was washed separately in the Sunday school room, numbered from 1 to 34 and prepared for examination before being returned to the main body of the church. Sergeant William Helsby, who was appointed mortuary keeper, said:

> I searched each of the bodies and all personal property was immediately listed and placed in an envelope and given the same number as the body. All clothing found on each of the victims was also listed and placed in a cloth bag; this too, was given the same number. I noticed while undertaking this task that all of the casualties had sustained serious injuries.
>
> On Saturday and Sunday 1st and 2nd March, I dispatched the bodies to Bolton Royal Infirmary, Bolton and District General Hospital and Westhoughton Mortuary, where post mortem examinations were performed, after which all the victims were returned to me at Victoria Methodist Church. On Sunday 2nd March, I received the body of Mr Partington, who had died in Bolton Royal Infirmary. Later that same day I was present when all the bodies, except Mr Tonkin, were placed in their coffins. Before each coffin was sealed I drew the undertaker's attention to the identifying mark on the body.
>
> On Monday 3rd March, I was present when the body of Mr Tonkin was placed in his coffin. At 10:45 am all the coffins, except those of Mr Adams and Mr Lindsay, were loaded on vehicles, which left at 12 noon en route for the Isle of Man.

Sheila Ashton has reason to remember that time. Her husband ran a DIY shop in Church Street, opposite the Victoria Road Methodist Church.

My husband supplied planks to lie across the pews and sheeting to cover the victims. He went across the road to help – I didn't go, but I remember later, when the planks were returned they were heavily bloodstained. It was awful. At the time the weather was very bad and Church Street was snowbound. My husband lit a sort of beacon fire in the roadway to guide rescue helicopters to the crash site, but because of the fog they couldn't land. Later, when the relatives came over to identify loved ones we took them in and gave them tea and sympathy. It was all so tragic. We did what we could.

Don Hulme, a 22-year-old police constable based in Horwich, spent the next 24 hours on duty at the church. He said:

I remember the weather on the day prior to the disaster was horrendous. The snow was falling heavily and I recall that during the early evening I was stationed at the Crown Hotel on Chorley New Road, Horwich, diverting traffic down Crown Lane to the A6 Blackrod By-pass, as Chorley New Road was virtually closed. Later that same evening I was stationed on the Blackrod By-pass diverting traffic back down Crown Lane due to the change in road conditions. Eventually the By-pass became completely blocked and I actually walked on the roofs of a number of vehicles, due to the depth of snow.

The following day I was asleep in my lodgings in Horwich, when I was awakened by the sound of emergency vehicle sirens passing by. When I was informed that an aircraft had crashed on Winter Hill I went directly to Horwich Police Station. I spent the next 24 hours on duty at the Methodist Church, which was used as a temporary mortuary for the victims.

The bodies of those persons so tragically killed were brought from the crash site and we placed them on stretchers, which were laid across the pews. The following hours were spent ensuring that the dead were made presentable and that all items of clothing and personal property were correctly recorded with a view to identification. All bodies were labelled either fit for identification or, identification by property only. This was extremely important, as not all the persons named on the flight manifest were actually on the aircraft. Furthermore, others not named had taken their place.

It must have been about 2 am, when a call came from the crash site asking if a check could be made of the bodies as what was believed to be an arm or a leg had been found amongst the wreckage. I was given the task of checking the bodies. I went into the church and thought little of it until I reached the far end, and then realised that there was only me in the darkened building and at least 30 bodies, with only half of them checked. Strangely enough I wasn't scared or frightened, as the press have reported, although I must say I was a little hesitant checking the rest. Despite talk of limbs being widely scattered, this was not the case. Only one of the deceased had lost a hand and this was placed with the body.

I think it was the following day, Saturday, 29 February, that I met Sergeant Bill Brown from the Isle of Man Constabulary. He had been sent over to liaise with the Lancashire Constabulary, firstly, because his father, Norman Hull Brown had been killed in the crash and secondly because he knew almost all of the passengers on the aircraft.

I spent a couple of days the following week at the crash

site, in the Lancashire Constabulary Control Vehicle and on other occasions on follow up enquires. That was my total involvement in the incident.

People have asked me how I coped. But back then you just got on with it. There was no counselling – nothing like there is today. It is not something you want to talk about really. Now I try not to think about it.

Sergeant Bill Brown, who Don mentions above, was a great help in easing the strain on the relatives, both during the inquest and at the identification. His son, John Brown told me:

My grandfather, Norman Hull Brown, ran a transport business with a garage in the Isle of Man, including coaches, wagons and general repairs. He was particularly keen to participate in the day trip as the Exide Factory, which was to be visited, was built on land formerly belonging to the farm on which he was brought up.

My father, William Hull Brown – known as Bill – was at the time a local police sergeant and because he was recovering from a hernia operation he found himself on the front desk in the main police station in Douglas. As a result he took the telephone call, which effectively informed the Island of the accident.

Strangely, about an hour before the notification, my grandmother, who lived in a very isolated property outside of Onchan, had telephoned my father to tell him that my grandfather's dog – a black and white spaniel called Rex – had gone berserk!

I was in primary school on the day and was informed of the accident by my teacher, Mrs Bridge, and then taken home. I vividly remember spending the late afternoon and evening travelling around the Island with my father, visiting the homes of the passengers, most of whom were very well known to our family.

Next day, my father travelled to Horwich with Harry Crennell and Olive Moore and subsequently formally identified the majority of the dead. Thereafter, he travelled home in a chartered plane with the coffins and, as was the way in those days, returned to work that evening – no question of counselling in 1958.

Because my grandfather was seventy years of age at the time of his death, the compensation received by my grandmother was negligible and following the accident my father took on responsibility for her.

It is difficult to convey the impact of this accident on the Island, which at that time was a very close local community. It was not until the 1970s that the Finance Industry really started taking hold here and we saw the fairly dramatic increase in population and the dilution of the local identity.

Another police officer involved with the aftermath was Patrick Wilson, for him the disaster made a lasting impression. He told researcher Paul Lomax:

In 1958, Horwich, and all towns and villages bordering Bolton were policed by the then Lancashire Constabulary; Bolton itself had its own Borough Police Force. At the time of the aircrash I was stationed in Farnworth. I and other officers from all sections of the Bolton Division of the Lancashire Police were sent to Horwich to assist as required.

I remember by the time I arrived at Horwich all the survivors had been taken to hospital, and the bodies of the victims, or at least what could be found, had been taken to a chapel, which was next door to the police station. Identification was a major problem; obviously we didn't have any DNA or other methods now available. Albeit that I completed 30 years in the Police Force – 24 years of which was in the CID, and as a Detective Chief Inspector have visited the scene of many murders. I still remember visiting that chapel, for some reason it is something that I have never forgotten. A macabre jigsaw would be the only way I could possibly describe it.

My duties from that time on were guarding the crash scene. At the time of the accident access to the site was difficult due to the snow, but during the following few days it became more accessible. The crash site itself was on the fringe of the hill on the Belmont side of the television mast. The wreckage was spread across the moorland. I remember quite distinctly that the tail section, although somewhat disjointed, was comparatively intact. I cannot remember exactly how long I was engaged looking after the scene, but it was quite a few days.

On a more personal note, but still involving the crash, concerns my father who was a time served soldier and had a love of good fountain pens and wristwatches. When I joined the regular army and was due to be posted to the Middle East, he asked me to see if I could find him a 'West End' watch. Apparently it was one of the best watches he'd ever had – his had been stolen. Although I searched and searched I could never find one.

Whilst I was at the scene of the crash on Winter Hill, I found a watch, and yes, it was a 'West End' – stopped at the exact time of the crash. I have never come across one since. I handed the watch in at Horwich Police Station at the end of my tour of duty together with another find – the top of someone's head. The injuries to the unfortunate victims were horrendous. It is nothing short of miraculous that anyone survived at all.

An unfortunate aftermath of the disaster were reports that souvenir hunters and looters had made their way to the unguarded crash site after darkness fell. The people of Horwich and Bolton were rightly indignant at the television news reports – ironically transmitted from Winter Hill – stating that souvenir hunters and scavengers had made their way to Winter Hill on the evening of the crash. Residents in Georges Lane spoke of a stream of cars and motorbikes going past in the dark. At the transmitter station, engineers said that about 20 or 30 people were at the scene of the crash at 8:00 pm. 'There were a lot of kids, some men and one woman,' said one of the engineers, 'taking anything they could find. The police had gone away but they came back quickly enough after our broadcast went out.'

A Horwich police officer that went to the scene immediately in response to the reports said: 'There was nobody there at 11 pm when I arrived, although I met a few people on their way down.' According to the police no guard was left at the scene because in the case of civil aviation accidents the responsibility of the police ceased when all the injured were safe and the bodies of the victims removed. Thankfully that situation does not exist today.

The newspapers the following day also highlighted the reports of scavengers at the scene. The press reports invoked strong feelings of disgust amongst the locals that people could be so morbid minded as to want souvenirs of such a tragic event, and that the activities of a minority should be given such emphasis by the media. None of the newspaper reports did justice to the heroic efforts made by local people in the rescue operations. The majority of those who climbed Winter Hill in the appalling conditions went up to help and assist as best as they could and their efforts far outweighed the ghouls who were drawn irresistibly to the disaster scene.

During the weekend many sightseers, the majority from outside the district, flocked to Winter Hill, but they found police preventing their cars from using the access road to the transmitter station. Those who tried to make their way there on foot over the moors found other police officers guarding the wreckage.

Throughout the day of the disaster the news began to slowly filter back to the Isle of Man where anxious relatives and friends waited for information. Along the promenade at Douglas, knots of people gathered and talked of the disaster or leaned over the shoulders of others to read the evening paper, their faces blank with disbelief. In the public houses, which were open all day, it was the same. Flags flew at half-mast, and there was an atmosphere of mourning all across the island. By nightfall the names of those who had perished totalled 35. The victims were mostly young, between the ages of 20 and 30 with wives and young children. Many of them had only recently been married. That day 27 wives lost husbands and 33 children, some whom had not yet been born, became fatherless.

Dorothy Howarth (now Asling) with her husband Malcolm. *(Dorothy Asling)*

Dorothy Howarth, who was pregnant with her son, was one of those wives anxiously waiting for news of her husband, Malcolm. She said:

Mac was 25 and we had been married exactly six months to that very day. He just went off that morning never to return home. I should have been with him to go shopping in Manchester, but I didn't feel up to it.

At the time we lived with his mother. I remember walking to the butchers that morning to buy two pieces of steak for our tea. As I entered the shop the butcher was talking to other people about the terrible plane crash that morning. I flippantly remarked that my husband was on a plane that morning on a trip to Manchester. He suddenly realised what he was saying and said: 'It's not the charter flight, it's the scheduled flight that's gone down.'

As I walked back I knew something was wrong. When I got to his mother's house she was on the telephone. But the thing about it was the co-pilot's name was also Howarth and he survived. Every time I rang Bolton Royal Infirmary for news they said: 'Oh yes, Mr Howarth from Royal Avenue, he's alive.' The police came five times to tell me – 'Dorothy no, Mac is dead.' I said, 'No, I'm sorry; he's in Bolton Infirmary.' But he wasn't. It was the co-pilot. Mac was dead.

One of the victims, Selwyn Lace, did not have a ticket for the flight over to Manchester, but took the place of another passenger at the last minute. Consequently, his name was omitted from the official list of the dead. His sister, Olga Grey was 21 and living in Liverpool at the time. She recalled:

Selwyn went from the Empire Garage in Peel. I think it was Dickie Craine who couldn't go so a coin was tossed and Selwyn got the seat. So my brother's name was not on the original list. It was Dickie's name instead.

I was asked to meet people off the boat – I don't think many flew over. Somebody said: 'Your brother's name is not on the list', but I had had a call from him to say he was going on the trip. They had turned the local Methodist church into a mortuary. I identified Selwyn's body. He had died instantly and I have never forgotten that you could see it had been absolutely sudden, like a clap on his chest. His eyes were open.

People were just everywhere. There were ladies making cups of tea. Nobody really knew what he or she was doing. There was no counselling, like there would be today, and none of the ancillary services we have now. But the people themselves were very kind. Every time I smell that dusty church smell, or the taste of tea in soapy cups, I go right back there.

Naturally, because of the enormity of the disaster there was extensive media interest in the story and journalists were immediately dispatched to cover every aspect of the accident. Ron Smith was a young reporter based in Liverpool at the time and within hours of the crash found himself on a plane flying to the Isle of Man. He told me:

In a chequered journalistic career spanning more than half a century, and embracing newspapers, radio, television and public relations, some days will inevitably stand out in the memory forever. Such a day was February 27, 1958, the day of the Winter Hill air crash, which killed 35 motor traders from the Isle of Man.

At the then age of 24, I had spent just a few months working alongside journalists much more experienced and senior than me, on the tabloid Liverpool Evening Express which, unbeknown to me at that time, was to close down within the next two years.

I was undertaking a dual role on the paper, covering the Liverpool Criminal Courts in the morning and the Municipal Council and Committee meetings in the afternoon.

I had returned from one of the courts at lunchtime on February 27, to be told by my News Editor that I was going to the Isle of Man because of the Winter Hill air crash that morning. The conversation between my News Editor and me was curt and to the point. 'When?' 'Now,' 'How?' 'A plane is standing by at Speke Airport.' 'How long will I be there?' 'As long as it takes. Maybe two or three days.' 'Can I go home for my razor and pyjamas?' 'No. Buy some throw away razors and sleep in your underpants.'

A car rushed me to the airport where I met a fellow reporter from the Liverpool Echo, sister paper of the Express but in direct editorial competition. On the runway was an old Rapide belonging to a company called Federated Fruiterers, which shuttled between Liverpool and Ireland most days with cargoes of mushrooms. In consequence there were no seats in the plane but two flimsy wooden dining room chairs had been provided for my colleague and me. We were both quite broadly shouldered and had to be shoehorned into the plane to sit shoulder to shoulder to canvas sides in the tiny aircraft. Bundles of the early afternoon editions of both the Evening Express and the Echo, containing the first reports of the Winter Hill crash, were also loaded onboard.

When the pilot arrived on a bicycle, wearing a green beret, sports jacket and bicycle clips, for me, making my first ever flight and to cover, above all things, an air disaster, neither the plane nor the pilot pointed to the most auspicious of days. The fact that the plane then flew into a strong, head on wind making it a slow and choppy flight did not help to settle either the nerves or stomach. Neither did the fact that the runway at Ronaldsway Airport began almost at the cliffs' edge and our approach, to a first time flyer like myself, the cliffs looked frighteningly beckoning. No doubt the pilot had witnessed this countless times and touched down safely.

My colleague and I had each been instructed by our news desk to file a story immediately we touched down. On the journey over, we had turned our backs on each other and scribbled away in our notebooks so as not to see what the other was writing. It was inevitable, however, that our stories were similar, the main theme being that we had flown into the Isle of Man with the very first copies of OUR newspaper telling the FIRST story of the disaster at Winter Hill. The upshot was that later that day we each got a rocket from our News Editor for 'collaborating over the stories.'

Quickly installed in a Douglas hotel, with throw away razors and prepared to sleep scantily clad, we joined 'the pack' – journalists from the national newspapers from London and Manchester – to attend briefings from the Governor's office and the police and, if possible, interview the families and friends of those who died at Winter Hill. If my memory serves me correctly, the relatives were well protected from 'the pack' by the authorities and most stories came from official sources. What I do remember distinctly, is that the reporter from the Daily Mirror spent most of his time in the hotel, as the Mirror, round that time, had issued a directive to all its reporters 'not to intrude upon private grief.'

After three days, in which the news media gave extensive coverage to the Winter Hill air crash, my colleague and I were called back to Liverpool – this time flying via Blackpool Airport in style in a Heron belonging to, or on loan to the management of Silver City Airways, owners of the ill fated Bristol Wayfarer.

Although some aspects of my own experiences in those

days nearly 50 years ago, are naturally a little vague, the overall memory of the Winter Hill air disaster – the location of which I see most days on my travels around the nearby Wigan area – has lived with me ever since and will no doubt continue to do so for the rest of my life.

# CHAPTER SIX

# PYRAMID OF CIRCUMSTANCES

*'First Officer Howarth's mistake was a gravely negligent act.'*
Commissioner John Megaw QC

On the day following the accident Arthur Broomfield, a Senior Investigating Officer of the Accident Investigation Branch, Farnborough, visited the scene and immediately began work to discover the cause of the crash. The wreckage distribution and impact marks on the ground were plotted and indicated that the aircraft had flown into the northern slope of Winter Hill at a height of approximately 1,440-1,450 feet above sea level. From the examination of a number of wristwatches recovered, it was established that the time of the crash occurred at between 9:44 and 9:45 am. Inspection of the two propellers indicated that both engines were under power at the time of impact ruling out any pre-crash malfunction. Once the on-site investigation was completed the wreckage was dragged off the hillside, loaded onto lorries and transported to the Ministry of Transport and Civil Aviation hangar at Speke Airport, Liverpool for further examination.

From the outset it was suspected that a navigational error was the cause of the accident, because Charlie Sierra, on its intended course to the Wigan Beacon should have been no closer than 7 miles from Winter Hill. To test this theory the radio compass and the direction finding loop aerial were removed for detailed examination. It was found that the setting on the tuning scale of the compass was 344 kilocycles, which is the Oldham Beacon frequency. Moreover, the position of the loop aerial and the reading of the bearing indicator were consistent with the radio compass having been set on the Oldham Beacon and not Wigan at the time of the crash.

This much was known when the Public Inquiry into the causes and circumstances of the accident was held at Holborn Town Hall, London, on 12, 13, 16 and 17 June 1958. John Megaw QC was appointed Commissioner with Captain Thomas Nisbet DFC and Captain Ian Wallace DFM as Assessors.

On the first day the inquiry room was filled to capacity and amongst the observers present were representatives of those who had lost their lives in the accident. Evidence was given from the Accidents Investigation Branch, Farnborough; Manx Airlines; Silver City Airways; Air Traffic Control Officers; eyewitnesses and experts from every aspect of aviation. In all, 24 witnesses would be called upon to give evidence.

Each day the evidence was heard and every known fact and relevant detail was brought out regarding that last flight of Charlie Sierra. Two matters that were brought up in the proceedings – although it was clear that they were in no way contributory to the accident but nevertheless gave the court cause for concern – were pertaining to the ballasting of the aircraft and the load and trim sheets.

There was much confusion as to how much and where the ballast was placed on the aircraft prior to the flight. Evidence was given by Kevin Skillicorn, a traffic clerk employed by Manx Airlines. He said that on the afternoon preceding the flight he was told by Captain Cairnes to arrange for 600lb of ballast to be put in the nose of the aircraft. This was on the assumption that 45 passengers would be on the flight. On the following morning, when only 39 passengers arrived, it was arranged with Captain Cairnes to transfer 150lb to the rear. Captain Cairnes said in his evidence that Mr Skillicorn went to see the engineers about this transfer.

When Mr Skillicorn prepared the load and trim sheets immediately before departure, he showed 450lb of ballast in the forward hold and

150lb in the rear, stowed under the seats of row 13. Mr Skillicorn himself had nothing to do with the actual placing of the ballast in the aircraft.

Mr O'Kane, an engineer with Manx Airlines, said that he was told by telephone on the afternoon of 26 February to load 350 to 400lb of ballast on the aircraft. He gave instructions accordingly to Mr Faragher, an Engineer Engine Fitter, who placed the ballast in the rear of the aircraft overnight. The following morning he moved the ballast as instructed to the forward hold. It consisted of three 50lb steel bars on the port side and three 50lb bars on the starboard side and a 75lb bar also in the forward hold – 375lb in total.

When Captain Cairnes checked the aircraft on the morning of the flight, he asked Mr Faragher if there was any ballast in the tail. Mr Faragher said 'No.' Captain Cairnes then instructed him to transfer the 75lb bar to the tail, underneath the hostess's seat.

First Officer, Bill Howarth said in his evidence that it was his duty as First Officer to see how much ballast had been loaded. He said he saw, but now cannot remember the amount, but recalled that the ballast was not secured when he last saw it. The reason he gave for this was that 'we were rather late in getting away'.

Captain Cairnes's recollection is very different from Mr Skillicorn's and Mr Faragher's recollection. He thought that on the previous day he told the engineers to put about 500lb in the nose. On the morning of the flight, as he entered the aircraft, he saw two engineers struggling up the gangway with a steel bar of ballast. He asked what were they doing. They said, 'We found this in the tail.' Captain Cairnes said, 'See there is no more.' He then looked at the ballast himself; he saw one long piece and three or four short pieces, none of which was secured because there was no rope available for lashing, but they were firmly wedged hard up against the bulkhead and the heating pipe, 'and nothing short of high turbulence would have shifted that ballast'.

It was impossible to ascertain from the examination of the wreckage at the crash scene exactly how much ballast was actually on board or where it was placed. Only one bar of 75lb, one bar of 50lb, and a portion of a bar weighing 12lb were recovered. It is probable that the remainder of the ballast had been flung out of the aircraft on impact. Those missing bars of ballast are probably today still embedded deep in the peat of Winter Hill.

Just prior to the take-off, Captain Cairnes signed the load and trim sheet, which showed 150lb of ballast in the tail of the aircraft under the hostess's seat. It is possible he didn't notice this statement on the document. If it were true it would have been a serious matter; since an unlashed steel bar in that position could have been a grave menace to the safety of the aircraft and its passengers. In the end the court was prepared to accept Captain Cairnes's version to the extent that all the ballast was in fact placed in the forward hold, but the court was not prepared to accept that the ballast was firmly secured. The fact of wedging the bars under the heating pipe could not be accepted as adequate securing. It was Captain Cairnes's duty, as laid down in the Air Navigation Order 1954, to satisfy himself 'that the load carried by the aircraft is of such weight, and so distributed and secured, that it may safely be carried on the proposed flight'. The Commissioner said, 'The excuses of lack of rope or lateness of take off are not acceptable.'

The Inquiry then went on to examine the inaccuracies in the load and trim sheets. Mr Skillicorn was responsible for preparing these documents for the flight. This task, for obvious reasons, had to be carried out shortly before take-off when the exact details of the number of passengers travelling are known. Mr Skillicorn prepared the load and trim sheets between 8:40 am when he arrived at the airport and 9:00 am. It was inaccurate in several respects. The total weight of the aircraft was wrongly calculated, though not to any serious degree. The exact extent of the error depends on the facts, which will never be known, as to the actual amount of ballast on board. To some extent this was not Mr Skillicorn's fault, since he did not have available the correct information regarding the empty weight of the aircraft.

But, more serious were Mr Skillicorn's admitted errors in preparing the graph on the right hand side of the load and trim sheet, by means of which the centre of gravity – the trim of the aircraft fore and aft – was calculated. Here he made a number of mistakes, including the omission from the calculation of one row of passengers. Luckily, his error was within the limits of the safe centre of gravity range of the aircraft. Captain Cairnes countersigned the inaccurate load and trim sheet, failing to notice these errors.

The Commissioner then dealt with the main thrust of the Inquiry – the setting of the radio compass by Bill Howarth. John Megaw said:

During Captain Cairnes' absence Mr Howarth set the radio compass – setting it, as he thought on Wigan Beacon, but, in fact, as must now be accepted beyond doubt, on Oldham Beacon. There can be little doubt that Mr Howarth, when he tuned in the radio compass looked, as he says he did, at the appropriate page in the Aerad Flight Guide, in order to find the frequency and identification signal of the beacon to which he intended to tune. If he had looked correctly at the entries opposite Wigan, he would have found that the frequency was 316, and the recognition signal MYK. If he had set the tuning scale to 316, he would have received signals from Wigan, and not Oldham, and he would have heard the recognition signal MYK, whereas, if he had tuned on Oldham and listened for the recognition signal, he would have heard the signal MYL. The letter K in morse is dash dot dash; the letter L is dot dash dot dot; and no one with experience of morse code should have confused the two. Of course, if he had failed to listen for that last letter of the call-sign – which would have been a grave error – he would have heard only the letters MY in morse, and those are the first two letters of both beacons.

There is no doubt that Mr Howarth for some reason in fact tuned the radio compass to Oldham Beacon. Mr Howarth frankly admits, in the light of what he now knows, that he must have done so. That in fact the radio compass was tuned to Oldham Beacon is shown conclusively by what was found on the examination of the wreckage after the accident.

It is necessary to consider what explanation there may be as to how the mistake was made, and what degree of blame is to be attached to Mr Howarth. First, as to the possible explanations. Mr Howarth was quite unable to give any real explanation. His evidence on this matter is as follows:

In examination by Counsel for the Attorney General:

Q     Did you tune in to 316?

A     I do not know. I think I probably tuned in to 344.

Q     If you did, of course, that would account very largely for this accident, would it not?

A     Yes.

Q     Oldham does not come into this flight at all, does it?

A     No.

Q     How do you think you came to tune in to 344?

A     Well, I was looking up and down at the guide on my knee, looking out of the window to see where I was going, and then looking up at the instrument, and I probably looked twice and skipped a line or something and deliberately tuned Oldham.

Q     You are conscious now, looking back, that you deliberately tuned in to 344 thinking it was Wigan?

A     No. I do not know that I did, but that is what I think from the evidence.

Q    Maybe I can shorten this. Looking back on it now, have you got any doubt really in your mind that you in fact tuned in to 344?

A    I do not really know what I tuned in to. I just think that I must have tuned to 344, but I did intend to tune to 316.

The Commissioner:

Q    You intended to tune to Wigan?

A    I intended to tune to Wigan, yes.

Q    What are you saying now; that you think you must have, or may have, tuned to 344, is entirely based on what happened afterwards?

A    Yes.

Q    When you tuned in you actually heard, did you, the call sign?

A    Yes.

Q    You listened for it?

A    Yes.

Q    What were you listening for?

A    If I had selected the Oldham frequency I would also select the Oldham call sign and if I heard it I would be quite satisfied.

Q    Then you would be listening for MYL?

A    Yes.

Q       Do you remember what you were listening for?

A       No.

In cross-examination by Counsel who represented him:

Q       Do you think the most likely thing is that you must perhaps, being distracted, have picked out the wrong frequency and the wrong call sign?

A       Yes.

Q       Rather than that you picked out the right one but put it on the set wrongly?

A       I am not likely to confuse the morse letters.

Q       I was going to ask you – do you think if you had done you would, with your knowledge of morse code, have confused one letter for another in listening to the call sign?

A       No, I am sure I would not.

The Commissioner continued:

> I am unable to accept the suggestion that the error arose as a result of Mr Howarth's eye 'skipping a line' when looking at the Aerad Flight Guide – three lines separate Oldham and Wigan. Nor am I able to accept the suggestion that he looked at the Wigan entry, saw the call sign MYK, then had his attention diverted by something, and, looking back at the guide, picked up the recognition signal MYL (Oldham), and, because of its similarity to the Wigan signal MYK, followed through that line of the guide and tuned in on the Oldham frequency. The most probable explanation, as it seems to me, is that Mr

Howarth, without realising it, had in his mind some, subconscious association between Oldham and Wigan; and that therefore, in looking at the guide and running his eye down the page, when he saw the name Oldham he momentarily assumed that was the place which he required, and therefore deliberately, although not realising that he had made this mistake, took the Oldham frequency from the guide and tuned in the radio compass to the Oldham frequency; and took the Oldham recognition signal from the guide and heard the very recognition signal which he expected to hear.

This theory, to some degree is strengthened by, first, Bill Howarth's conversation with Alan Sucksmith, one of the engineers at the transmitter station shortly after the crash, when he certainly took the initiative in mentioning Oldham and secondly, by his statement to Mr Trench, Inspector of Accidents, made in Bolton Royal Infirmary the day after the accident, when, on being asked 'Which beacon would you go to in entering the Manchester Zone?' He replied 'I think you get Blackpool, Oldham, etc.'

The Commissioner, John Megaw, in summing up this evidence, said:

Mr Howarth's mistake must be regarded as a gravely negligent act. There is, of course, no question of any deliberate or intentional breach of duty. There is no question of any general attitude of recklessness in Mr Howarth's approach to his duties and responsibilities. It may well be that this was an isolated mistake on the part of a man who is not normally liable to make such mistakes, and who is, by nature, conscientious and careful. But when everything has been taken into account in his favour, I am driven to the conclusion that this error, which was the cause of the accident, must be described as default on the part of Mr Howarth.

The court then dealt with the failure of Air Traffic Control to give the aircraft the Barnsley QNH.

When Mr Lauderdale, the officer on duty at Preston Control gave Charlie Sierra clearance to enter the Manchester Control Zone, he did not give the Barnsley QNH, as the regulations required him to do. Mr Lauderdale said in his evidence to the inquiry that his decision not to pass on the Barnsley QNH, was deliberate, and that it was based on his own interpretation of the regulations.

It will always remain a matter of speculation, that if the Barnsley QNH had been passed to the aircraft, the accident could have been fortuitously avoided. The Barnsley QNH at the time was 1021 millibars. The Holyhead QNH, to which the altimeters of Charlie Sierra had been set on departure from Ronaldsway, was 1024 millibars. If Mike Cairnes had received the Barnsley QNH he would have reset his altimeters accordingly. That means from the Reporting Point onwards, the altimeters would have been set 3 millibars lower. One millibar's difference in setting makes a difference of approximately 30 feet in height, 3 millibars makes a difference of 90 feet.

If the altimeters on Charlie Sierra had been set 90 feet lower, Mike Cairnes, in attempting to maintain a height of 1,500 feet, would probably have been flying 90 feet higher than he actually was. The crash occurred at a height of approximately 1,460 feet. The summit of Winter Hill is 1,498 feet. The extra 90 feet of height given by the different setting of the altimeters would have resulted in Charlie Sierra clearing the summit of the hill with some 50 feet to spare. But, nevertheless, there was still the possibility of the aircraft striking the television mast.

'The primary responsibility for the QNH error,' said the Commissioner, 'lies with the Air Traffic Controller, Mr Lauderdale. However, Captain Cairnes must take some responsibility, since it was his duty to request the QNH if the Traffic Controller did not give it to him.' Mike Cairnes in his evidence said he did not notice that the QNH had not been given.

Was the accident contributed to by any wrongful act or default on the part of Captain Cairnes? The commissioner said there are two, and only two possible grounds on which such responsibility might be attributed to him. The first depends on the suggestion that he continued to fly on his supposed course after the weather conditions had become such that the condition of 'contact' given in the clearance by the controller was no longer being fulfilled. The second is that he had a duty to check that the radio compass was in fact tuned to the Wigan Beacon.

Dealing with the first point, regarding his continued flight in the worsening weather conditions and eventual loss of visual contact with the ground. The evidence showed that when the aircraft was in the position, which we now know – although the Captain did not know – over Chorley, it began to run into patches of cloud and rain. After that the weather conditions quickly deteriorated and the aircraft was soon completely enveloped in cloud. This sudden envelopment took place perhaps 10 or 15 seconds before 9:44 + 33 seconds, which was the time when Manchester Control sent the message 'Charlie Sierra are you in visual contact with the ground?' To which message the reply was 'Negative.' When that message was received the aircraft had only just been enveloped in cloud, and Captain Cairnes was expecting – and had possibly given some instruction by signs – that Bill Howarth should inform Manchester Control that 'contact' had been lost. Up to the moment of the sudden envelopment in cloud, Captain Cairnes had not, according to his interpretation of the phrase, lost 'contact'; since, apart from momentary obscuring by patches of cloud, he had not been prevented from seeing substantially the whole of the ground beneath him. The Commissioner said:

> If the facts as given by Captain Cairnes and Mr Howarth are right – and I accept them – then, on Captain Cairnes's interpretation of the terms of his clearance, he obeyed the instructions of that clearance.

> It will be borne in mind that Captain Cairnes was firmly under the impression that he was on a direct course to Wigan, and it never crossed his mind that he could be less than about seven miles from Winter Hill. He was waiting for Wigan Beacon to show on the needle of the radio compass, and he was from moment to moment expecting the needle to swing round,

showing that he had crossed the beacon. It is clear that he did not know, from any observation of the ground, precisely where he was. Otherwise, when he passed over Chorley – assuming he could still see the ground – he must have recognised that he was already far off his course.

The Commissioner continued:

Of all the facts which I have accepted, and bearing in mind the doubt and ambiguity as to the meaning of the word 'contact' in clearances such as this, I acquit Captain Cairnes of blame in this respect of his continuing to fly for as long as he did without seeking further instructions from Manchester Control or reporting loss of contact, or taking other action. After he had reported loss of 'contact', the order to turn immediately followed; and it goes without saying that no blame attaches to Captain Cairnes for immediately complying with this order.

On the second point – his failure to check the setting of the radio compass. Mike Cairnes said that on his return to the cockpit, he assumed that the radio compass was tuned to the Wigan Beacon. He said that he looked at the magnetic compass, and that the course being flown appeared to him to be consistent with a course to Wigan. Thereafter he concentrated his attention on the radio compass. It is fair to say that one cannot in any case treat the magnetic compass as giving an accurate reading to within a few degrees. The difference between the radio compass and magnetic compass, when Mike Cairnes made his check, was not sufficiently large enough to make him come 'alive' from that check, to the possibility of an error in the tuning of the radio compass.

It does not follow, however, that he was right in not making any check of the setting of the radio compass, merely because the magnetic compass at the time gave no obvious indication of an erroneous setting of the radio compass.

The Commissioner, John Megaw QC, said of Captain Cairnes's

failure to check the radio compass setting:

When Captain Cairnes understood, some time before Charlie Sierra arrived at the Reporting Point, that Mr Howarth had set the radio compass on Wigan Beacon, he took no steps whatever to check the setting himself, other than to compare his radio compass course with the magnetic compass. He took no steps to ensure that Mr Howarth checked, or rechecked, the radio compass setting. It is at all times the duty of the Captain of an aircraft to ensure its safe navigation.

It may be too high a standard to lay down that a Captain should check every beacon tuned in by his First Officer. There are, however, certain occasions when it is the absolute duty of the person in command to check the identification of radio aids, and I am satisfied that this duty is understood and accepted in practice by all careful and competent pilots as a matter of good operating practice. For example, checking is required when making an instrument approach to land, or when flying in a Control Zone, or when flying below the minimum safe altitude for the area, or when the particular radio aid is the only navigational aid available and there is no means of effective cross-checking by reference to something else. At least two of these factors existed on this flight from the Reporting Point to Wigan. Captain Cairnes failed to check the radio compass setting, as he should have done. Had he done so, the mistake would have been detected and the accident prevented. I am accordingly driven to the conclusion that there was, in this case, default on the part of Captain Cairnes in failing to check that the radio compass was tuned on Wigan Beacon. That default contributed to the accident.

In light of the evidence that came out in the Inquiry, the Commissioner made several recommendations that should be acted upon.

It was thought that the position of the radio compass on the Wayfarer should be more conveniently positioned. On Charlie Sierra, the control unit was situated in the roof of the cockpit, above, and slightly behind the co-pilot's seat. It involves some difficulty for the First Officer to operate it, reaching over his left shoulder to the roof of the cockpit; and greater difficulty for the Captain to operate. It was suggested that the radio compass control should be more conveniently placed in the front of the cockpit, centrally above the windscreen. In this position the control box would be within comfortable reach of both the Captain and First Officer. The Commissioner said: 'This is a defect of no little importance and it should be remedied.'

He also dealt with the beacon recognition signals, which could cause possible confusion for pilots when setting the radio compass. He said:

> A number of navigational aid stations in the area in question have recognition signals beginning with the same letters, MY. I am unable to see any advantages, and I can see obvious disadvantages in this practice. It has been suggested that it may contribute to errors of identification. Why should not the letters of the recognition signals be made as different as possible, particularly for navigational aid stations in the same area? Would it not be better if the recognition signals bore some general identification with the names of the respective stations? For example, Wigan Beacon might be WIG or WGN. At the same time, it would undoubtedly be helpful if the rate of coding were to be increased. At the time of the accident, Wigan Beacon gave its recognition signal only twice in one minute. At a rate of coding of twice in one minute, the pilot seeking identification may have to wait for thirty seconds before he can identify the station. I should have thought that a rate of coding of less than six per minute was not really satisfactory. I strongly recommend that these matters be given urgent attention.

The resulting change of the beacon identification letters to reflect the beacon name probably prevented another similar accident.

The final outcome of the inquiry was damning for Bill Howarth. But was this lapse in airmanship on his part the single effective cause of the disaster? Having researched this accident in depth over the last five years, studied the mass of documentation that came out of the inquiry and undertook many interviews, I have come to the conclusion that there was no single cause for the accident. Although Bill Howarth bore the brunt of the blame in failing to set the radio compass correctly – a genuine error he freely admits – it is to my mind a 'pyramid of circumstances' in which, problem after problem began to stack up throughout the flight, causing a chain of events that would ultimately put the aircraft into the side of Winter Hill.

It all began before take-off. If the flight had not been late in getting away that morning, and had kept to the scheduled departure time of 9:00 am, then quite likely the ADR159 airway would have been clear of traffic and they would have been given their booked clearance of 3,500 feet all the way through on the route.

On reaching the Reporting Point off the coast Mike Cairnes was fully expecting to be cleared to a higher altitude before entering the Manchester Control Zone. That clearance was not given, as we know because a Silver City Airways Dakota piloted by Captain Skemp, was flying from Manchester to Blackpool at 2,500 feet, and approaching the Wigan Beacon and about to descend towards Squires Gate. There was the obvious danger, if the clearance had been given, that Charlie Sierra would cross its path.

It is possible that, if Mike Cairnes had actually known that there was low cloud in the vicinity of Winter Hill, he might have refused the clearance to enter the Zone at 1,500 feet and circled at the reporting point until he could be given a clearance at a higher altitude. It did not occur to him that on his assumed course to the Wigan Beacon he was likely to fly in the neighbourhood of high ground. On his proper course to Wigan Beacon, Winter Hill would never have been less than seven or eight miles distant. He accepted the clearance to enter the Manchester Control Zone at 1,500 feet as safe in the circumstances as he knew them.

Still, all was not lost. If, on entering the Manchester Control Zone, the controller had passed on to the aircraft the Barnsley QNH – which was his duty to do so – the crew would have reset their altimeters, and even though they were on the wrong course, would have probably, on the new altimeter setting, been flying the best part of 50 feet higher than the summit of Winter Hill. But as we know, the controller failed to pass on that vital information which could have saved the aircraft. Also, if the Decca Navigational Equipment had been set up before take-off, or during the early part of the flight, then both pilots would have seen on the Decca chart their true position and been alerted to the erroneous radio compass setting and altered their course before reaching the high ground of Winter Hill.

At this point the net finally began to close in on Charlie Sierra. But even now the crash was not inevitable. As the aircraft approached the area of Winter Hill it was flying above and along the valley to the north of the hill. On that course the aircraft would have cleared the high ground. But that final avenue of escape was blocked when the Manchester Controller gave the order to turn right. It was that instruction that finally sealed the fate of Charlie Sierra and its passengers and took the aircraft into the north east slope of Winter Hill.

If that order to turn had been delayed by just a few seconds, then Charlie Sierra would have cleared the crest of the hill safely. Thereafter there was no high ground on their flightpath and the visibility was much improved. Soon after, the crew would have realised their mistake and would have altered their course accordingly and landed safely at Manchester. The 39 motor traders would have enjoyed their day out in Manchester and returned to the Isle of Man later that evening to their homes and families, and Thursday, 27 February 1958 would have been just another uneventful day in British civil aviation history. Luck sometimes plays a part in aviation, and it can make the difference between life and death, but as we have seen, everything that could go wrong on that flight did. Fate, it seemed, was the hunter that day.

# CHAPTER SEVEN

# REFLECTIONS

*'It was like returning to an empty house.'*
Survivor, Fred Kennish

In a letter to this author in 1999, Survivor Fred Kennish told me of his thoughts and feelings some 40 years after the accident.

Six days after the crash I came round in Bolton Royal Infirmary and saw Jimmy Crosbie in the next bed. I thought we had had an accident in Manchester – I thought, trust us to have been hit by a bus! During my time in hospital I received the attention of the finest surgeons and staff that anyone could have wished for, and I thank them all. It was two months before I got back to the Isle of Man, by which time all of the funerals had taken place. For me it was like returning to an empty house.

I spent one night at home before I was sent away to Broadgreen Hospital in Liverpool to have my leg amputated. It was there that I met Mr Almond the surgeon. He asked me, 'Do you go to social evenings and like to dance?' I thought to myself, I'm in here to have my right leg removed at the hindquarter and he's talking about dancing! He must be mad! Anyway, he said he would like to try out an experiment to see if he could save my leg. I thought, what have I got to lose and

Fred Kennish and his wife Connie at Horwich Fire Station, shakes hands with his rescuer, Jimmy Arrowsmith - on the left retired fire officer John Lee. *(Bolton Evening News)*

Jimmy Arrowsmith & Fred Kennish return to Winter Hill. *(Bolton Evening News)*

told him to go ahead. Thankfully today I am still walking around on that leg.

I went back to the crash site a few years after the accident. I took some flowers and daffodil bulbs with me to see if they would grow on the mountainside. But the ground was so impregnated with oil that not even the grass would grow on that spot.

In 1989, Fred, as the elected Mayor of Douglas, made an emotional return to Winter Hill with his wife Connie. Fred explained:

I have always wanted to go back to see how bad it was. I always thought the Isle of Man should have done some thing at the time to honour the people of Bolton and Horwich for all they did. When I became Mayor I decided there was no better time.

During his visit he called in at the Bolton Royal Infirmary to remind staff that: 'I'm still around and thanks for everything.' The Mayor and Mayoress of Bolton also entertained the couple to dinner at the Town Hall. The following day, Fred and Connie called in at Horwich Fire Station to present a commemorative plaque and meet two of the firemen who were amongst the first to attend the scene. As he chatted to retired station officer John Lee and retired fireman Jimmy Arrowsmith, Fred recalled how he was left for dead at the scene, because it appeared that nothing could be done for him. Then Jimmy Arrowsmith chipped in and said:

I remember that. It was me and the late Dennis Howlett who picked you up; you were in a terrible state. The fog was so thick that day you had to stoop low to see anywhere. I found you on the ground in the snow with your arms crossed as if in the dying position, but I realised you were still alive.

The emotion was almost too much for Fred to bear when he realised that after all these years he had come face to face with one of the men who rescued him and effectively saved his life.

The Horwich firemen then drove Fred and his wife to the summit of Winter Hill – again in thick fog – for a few poignant moments near the spot where the aircraft crashed. With the help of Horwich Rotary Club he unveiled a plaque on the transmitter station building as a memorial to those who died and in gratitude to the people of Bolton and Horwich for the help they gave. Fred explained:

I feel I am part of Bolton as I have some of the town's blood in me – I needed a transfusion of about nine pints. The people of Bolton and Horwich were marvellous to me. I do recall some wonderful people helping me and the other survivors with their hospitality, giving us clothes, food and other treats. Strangers came to visit me as well as representatives from organisations like the Buffaloes and the RAF. I shall always have a soft spot for the town. I'll never be able to thank everyone enough. They were wonderful.

Forty-six years on – what are my feelings? The memories are all very sad; there is always this feeling of, why did I survive? All my mates … Every garage on the island had somebody on the trip. I'm the last one left of that group of motor traders, and I feel very much alone, whereas if the crash had not happened a lot of my friends would perhaps still be around today.

People say to me, you look really well. They don't know the half of the suffering over the last 40 odd years. In 1958, with having children, you had to get back to work or starve. There was no counselling or help from the government in those days. I still suffer from pain in my leg, spine and shoulders, but that is a small price to pay for seeing your children grow up.

A few years ago I was in Spain, and by coincidence met the pilot, Captain Cairnes. His legs were in a terrible mess and he's had it rough since the accident; in fact I felt pity for him. As for Bill Howarth, the co-pilot, I have not met him. I would just like to say to him – thanks for walking in the right direction that morning for help.

I think my only achievements have been becoming a councillor of Douglas Corporation and being elected Mayor of the town in 1989. This helped me in getting the plaque erected on the transmitter station - I hope the lads on Winter Hill approve.

Fred Kennish at Winter Hill as Mayor of Douglas. Inset: The memorial plaque.
*(Fred Kennish)*

Stewardess, Jennifer Curtis (now Fleet) told this author in 2001:

I was in hospital for ten days before we were flown back to the Isle of Man in a de Havilland Heron laid on by the airline. I was a bit anxious making that flight, but my father said to me, 'Jennifer, we live on a small island and you can't go back by boat because you suffer terribly from seasickness. Your mother and brother are waiting for you. You can't remain on the mainland for the rest of your life. You know you've got to get back in an aeroplane.' So that was it. With him sitting beside me I felt everything would be OK.

Six weeks after recovering from my injuries I was back on duty in a Bristol Wayfarer flying with passengers. I felt that returning to flying was a natural progression – getting on with life. Living on an island and knowing I get desperately seasick, I was going to have to fly off the island on a regular basis. Even just to buy clothes in Liverpool, which I used to do, because on the Isle of Man in those days you couldn't buy anything much. So I knew right from the start I would have to fly again.

The Author with Jennifer Curtis (now Fleet) at the Jolly Crofters on the 43rd anniversary. *(Author's collection)*

I do remember just feeling slightly anxious on that first flight on duty after the accident. The guy on the apron who accompanies the passengers out to the aircraft said:

'Nothing is going to happen to you this time is it Jennifer?' I said: 'No, you're right, it isn't.' With that he shut the door and thumped on the side of the aircraft for good luck. Once we had taxied out and gone past V2 on the take off run I was OK.

But her return to flying was not, however, without incident, as she recalls:

I remember once a porthole window blowing in as we were taxiing down the runway – I found that was pretty hairy. On another occasion we were about to land and we coming in lower and lower. Just as I thought we were about to touch down the engines screamed at full power and we climbed away – the Captain had aborted the landing. I got on the intercom and asked him what that was all about. He said: 'What you wouldn't have seen but we could, was a horse galloping down the runway centre line – we've just missed it!'

But the worst incident occurred when we were flying in a storm and about to land at Birmingham Airport. Suddenly the port engine was struck by lightening, exploded and flames shot out; it certainly rocked the aircraft quite a bit. Fortunately, the Captain was the Chief Pilot of the airline and very experienced and landed the aircraft safely. If it had been a younger pilot with not quite as much experience then we might not have been so lucky.

I continued flying right up until I got married on the Isle of Man in January 1959, and within a fortnight came to Manchester where I've lived ever since. Looking back now I don't think too much about the accident. It is always there at the back of my mind but I can remember distinctly after it happened that I really didn't want to talk about it. I wanted to dismiss it completely from my mind, and possibly that was a way of coming to terms in my own way as how to deal with it. I really did think that it would never happen to me again and I still do believe that I won't ever be involved in another plane crash. It is really only lately that I don't mind talking about it. I am amazed that people still remember it, as it happened such an awful long time ago and there have been other air disasters ten times worst than ours.

I remember the first time I took my baby daughter on a flight, I was going back to the Isle of Man to show her to my parents – she was only 3 months old. So it just shows that I wasn't against flying. I trusted the airline that I would arrive safely at my destination. Then I remember sending her as an unaccompanied minor to the Isle of Man, I told her to ask the stewardess if she could sit at the back. Right from the time when I thought she could understand, I told her I had been in an air crash. I would show her an aeroplane that was flying over our house and I would say, I was in something like that and we crashed. When my husband drove us in the direction of Winter Hill – not that we ever went up there – we would point and say that's where I crashed. So both my children from an early age weren't fearful of flying because their mother was alive and never made it sound a frightening thing.

I always believed that sitting at the back of the aircraft was the safest place, it certainly saved my life, and I'm very thankful that I was spared. I'm sorry for the other passengers who didn't survive.

For Mike Cairnes, his flying career ended on that bitterly cold February morning on Winter Hill. So severe were his injuries that it seemed he would not survive, let alone walk again. But having met and talked at length with Mike, his great strength of character and indomitable spirit shine through, and now in his eighties he still looks forward to the future. He had no hang-ups after the accident and didn't dwell on his disabilities; he just carried on and found something new to do. He told me:

I was operated on at Bolton Royal Infirmary and they did
very well because they didn't expect me to live. One
thing I did have was very good medical insurance, and
when that came through I was moved to the Lourdes
Hospital near Liverpool – largely due to my mother and
sister who were both nurses. The hospital was run by
nuns and had a superb operating theatre and wonderful
nursing.

When I arrived there I was wheeled in on the inevitable
trolley and once inside a broad Irish voice boomed out at
me – 'I'm the Matron don't yer know. Here, 'ave a drop
of this, it'll do yer the world of good.' She went over to
a statue of Our Lady and from a cupboard underneath
produced a bottle of whisky and a glass and goes glug,
glug, glug, glug glug, and passes me an absolute tumbler
full of whisky. I told her I didn't drink the stuff. She
said, 'It's the best medicine in the world.' So I took the
glass and drank a bit of that but couldn't drink it all.

The author with Mike Cairnes in 2002. *(Author's collection)*

During my stay there, the Grand National was on and all the nuns were allowed to bet up to half a crown on the race each year. When the race was broadcast I remember them cheering and cheering and shouting – Come on! Come on! Looking back now I think it was they who were largely responsible for how quickly I recovered. In all, I spent about two years in hospital, having six operations on my feet and legs.

Mike never lost either his courage or enthusiasm for flying. He continues:

After I came out of the Lourdes I flew my own car – which was stranded on the Isle of Man – to Blackpool in a Bristol Wayfarer. I knew the captain in command very well and he knew me. He said, 'Mike, it's your car, do you want to fly?' I had no hesitation taking the controls and flew the whole trip, take off, flying and landing. I would not hesitate to fly now – I love flying.

I always wanted to fly. I joined the RAF in 1939 and learnt to fly on a Blackburn B2 biplane. It was so old and slow it couldn't even keep up with a Tiger Moth. Then I was posted and did the last course on the Hawker Hart and Hawker Audax, beautiful Rolls-Royce Kestrel engined aircraft with all the power in the world. They had very long exhaust pipes to take the noise away behind you so that you could sit back and enjoy the scenery – a real gentleman's aeroplane.

I then did my advanced training on the Kestrel engined Miles Master then went onto Hawker Hurricanes patrolling the Pembrokeshire coast as far as Milford Haven. But I always wanted to fly bombers and when my posting came through I went on to Wellingtons and then Lancasters.

After the war things became a bit tight and through the

RAF benevolent fund got a job on the Berlin Air Lift flying a twin-engined Vickers Viking and then Avro Tudors with British South American Airways. I enjoyed the work on the Air Lift very much. After the Air Lift finished I stayed on with BSAA flying Avro Yorks on the South American routes.

I asked Mike if he was disappointed that because of his injuries he sustained in the Winter Hill accident he would never fly again.

No. Nothing worries me. I got a thousand pounds from the Winter Hill Disaster Fund and bought a little garage business in Herefordshire, which had a lovely old Elizabethan Manor house with it. I had a word with my surgeon and asked him if there was any point operating again, which he wanted to do. He told me that my ankles would never get any better and I might as well cease having further operations. He also told me that, as my ankles were 'fixed', I would never have any movement in them. So we decided to open the garage business and get cracking.

The business proved very good as this was a busy holiday road to South Wales and the petrol trade helped immensely. Because I had served my apprenticeship with Alvis, they gave me the distributorship for Herefordshire, Worcestershire and Radnorshire. About this time also, the distributorship for Peugeot became vacant and as a result I got this too.

The Peugeot became very popular with farmers in the area, but farmers do not take care of their vehicles and when the time came for them to trade in for a new Peugeot, their old one was probably battered and covered in muck. Consequently it was difficult to give them a good trade-in price. However, the business proved very satisfactory, although it was a strain to pay back the mortgage and it was very hard work.

About this time I was up a ladder one day repairing the roof when I noticed, and felt, my left ankle literally turn over. I struggled down the ladder, phoned my surgeon who told me to come in immediately. The result of this was that he could do nothing much about it apart from putting my left leg in irons and hoping this would straighten it. However, it did not have any effect and the leg swelled right up and I had to have one more operation in which the surgeon drilled right through the left ankle into the bones, so that the swelling would go down. I am now left with a permanent half-inch diameter drain hole, which I have to keep dressed every two days as it continually leaks. Out of it I sometimes get tiny bits of Bristol aeroplane!

I always wanted to motor race and have always been a keen follower of it. One day, a great friend of mine, and a customer, brought in his supercharged 8-litre Bentley Special, which he raced, and he kept on at me to take up motor racing with my rather special Alvis. This was a Vandan Plas open sports-tourer speed 20, into which I had fitted a speed 25 engine that I had highly tuned. This was a very quick motorcar indeed, so I entered it at Silverstone under the Historic Racing Car Class. To my amazement I came in third with relative ease, although I was up against Formula One, Maserati, the super-charged Bentley Special and a mass of racing Bugattis, to name a few.

I must mention that at first I had some difficulty, because of my disability, getting a racing licence. Eventually, after much discussion, the competition committee said, all right, you can have a competition licence, but you must carry your crutches in your car when racing! That was the most stupid thing I ever heard. I remember once racing at Silverstone and heard the voice of Raymond Baxter over the tannoy – he did the commentaries – 'Ah, there goes Mike Cairnes, he's thrown a crutch out at Copse, there'll be another soon.' I threw the bloody things out of course.

I raced the Alvis in the early 1960s for two seasons with reasonable success but never exceeding third place. So I decided to build an Alvis Special, building it from scratch as a racing car. I was a familiar sight, sitting on the floor, still in plaster, working, welding and machining. To do this I had to bring all the lathes, welding equipment etc. in the garage down to floor level. I had, as a basis, a very good Alvis Speed 20 saloon. I removed the body, chopped 18 inches out of the chassis and welded it up again with all the problems this entailed, removing all the excess equipment such as brackets for the running boards etc, until I had a very light short chassis. Onto this I put a body, which I had built from scrap pre-war Alvis cars.

The time was now approaching for the motor racing season to start, so I entered the Alvis Special at Oulton Park for a fairly long distance race and my partner in the business, who had done a lot of motor racing, drove this new one just to try it out, whilst I drove my original Alvis. To our amazement, the Special won the race! And considering we had only used the original Speed 20 engine – I thought that this was amazing. As a result of this success, I decided to really go to town on the Special and fitted a 4.3 litre Alvis engine – again pre-war. By this time I had already gained a reputation for tuning Alvis engines, and even had a customer from the United States.

I drove this car with great success for about five seasons, but in motor racing you have to improve the car each year and I was just about getting to the limit. When I took it down to the rolling-road-break in Worcestershire where the BRM team were having their cars tested, the engineer in charge asked me what b.h.p. I expected at the wheels. I said about 160. He said then you would not need a car pulling you backwards all the time to keep you on the rollers. However, he told me to just drive normally as you would when racing. So I set off on the rollers until I was getting maximum revs in third gear when he came up in front waving red flags shouting – 'Stop'! He said you're way over 200 already; you will need a car pulling you backwards to stay on the rollers. The BRM team, who were standing around looking very interested, said they'd do it. So they connected their estate car up and off we went again. To my amazement I got just over 280-horse power at the wheels!

As the years went by, the business sadly deteriorated – this was mainly due to the fact that road development and by-pass schemes affected the traffic, which in turn affected petrol sales, almost cutting my sales in half. Also BMC bought up Alvis and Rover, and the Alvis name disappeared from the map altogether. Due to these circumstances I decided to sell the business, which I got a good offer for, and it was turned into a transport café and hostel.

When the sale was completed, my wife and I then decided to buy a boat in Dartmouth, Devon, which needed a lot of work on it, so we lived in a caravan and spent four years rebuilding the boat which was in dry dock.

When we had completed all the work on the boat, we put it in the water at Dartmouth Harbour. We sold the caravan and started to live on the boat, making the final adjustments to it. After about nine months we set sail, first to Weymouth, and then from Weymouth to the River Seine in France. As we were approaching the narrow part of the English Channel, a British Destroyer stopped us. An officer on board raised his loudhailer but no sound came. I replied to the silence with my loudhailer, which was on top of the mast, saying – 'I think you'd do better if you switched it on!' The red-faced officer then said: 'Where from, wither bound.' I replied, 'Dartmouth to the Med., stopping on the way at various harbours.' He then asked me if I had any immigrants on board, to which I replied no. We then went on our way without further ado.

During our journey up the River Seine, we put into an official mooring place for the night, only to be confronted by lots of boats, including one British boat where a man dressed in full Highland regalia and playing the bagpipes. He then stopped playing and said to us through a hailer, 'Come and moor alongside me. Any boat with the name *Siryadh* is welcome.' As we had never known what the name meant, we asked him why he was interested. He said *Siryadh* is Gaelic for Water Wanderer. It turned out that this man had a free mooring, permanently paid for by the local mayor, provided that every weekend he dressed up and played the bagpipes, which was good for the tourist trade.

We continued slowly on our travels, stopping here and there at various interesting places, taking many months to reach the Med which we entered at Sette in France. We then continued down the coast of France to Spain and eventually came to settle in the international Marina of Torrevieja. We liked the area so much and made lots of good friends, that we decided to buy a bungalow and settle down permanently.

Mike knows that he shoulders some of the blame for the accident and doesn't shirk that responsibility, he told me: 'As Captain of the aircraft you have to bear that portion of the blame, which a Captain always does, whatever the outcome.'

Mike is now settled in the sunnier climes of Spain with his wife Sue, where he works on his boat and is contemplating writing his memoirs of what has been without doubt an extraordinary life.

Bill Howarth, who bore the brunt of the blame for the accident was suspended from civil flying for a short time and became a flying instructor. He then went on to fly Bristol Wayfarers again before joining Aer Lingus in 1960. During his time with the airline he flew the F27 Friendship, Vickers Viscount and BAC One-Eleven jet airliners, and for two periods as training Captain on Short 3-30 and 3-60 aircraft. During his off-duty hours in the summer months he flew the 1936 vintage DH89 Dragon – a wooden framed, plywood and canvas skinned biplane – at air displays throughout the UK. He retired from Aer Lingus in 1990 having served with them without incident for 30 years. He now lives in County Dublin.

Bill Howarth as Senior Captain with Aer Lingus. This photograph was taken after his last wth the airline in 1990. *(Bill Howarth)*

Alan Sucksmith, one of the few surviving engineers, on duty at the transmitting station on the day of the crash now lives in retirement in Cumbria. He told me:

I remained with the ITA – later the IBA – for the next thirty years or so, being posted to various TV transmitter sites around the country, including the Isle of Wight, Winter Hill again as Assistant Engineer in Charge, Belmont in Lincolnshire, and finally as Area Engineer for the Borders, based at Caldbeck in Cumbria. In this role I was responsible for the maintenance of the main and the many relay stations in Cumbria and the south of Scotland, and some six stations on the Isle of Man. I used to visit the Island once or twice a year.

Rather than relocate after twenty years in Cumbria, I took early retirement from the IBA when it reorganised at the end of 1988. I then, as a sort of retirement job, spent quite a happy six years looking after the technical facilities at the Nurse Training School at the Cumberland Infirmary in Carlisle, with added responsibilities at the

Nurse Training Schools in Whitehaven, Barrow and Lancaster. I left when Nurse Training was reorganised – but by then I was 63!

John Hall, the only other surviving engineer, now living in Leicestershire, told me:

I joined the ITA as Shift Engineer at Winter Hill in 1957. The air crash in 1958 prompted me to apply for the post of Shift Engineer at Mendlesham in Suffolk, when the station opened in late 1959. In March 1969 I was promoted to Senior Shift Engineer at Black Mountain in Northern Ireland. Shortly after this the Province troubles started. I was involved in the maintenance of the transmitting stations over the whole of Northern Ireland, including Strabane, near Londonderry. We had many close calls and one of our link relay stations was blown up.

John Hall.
*(Bolton Evening News)*

My family, consisting of my wife and three young children, had to live for three years in this turmoil before we were given a chance of transferring back to the mainland. I chose Emley Moor, near Huddersfield, where I started as Senior Shift Engineer in 1972. I was offered a post back to Northern Ireland in charge of all the transmitting stations, but my wife refused to go back. I retired in 1990.

In 1998, as the 40th anniversary approached memories of the disaster were evoked again. In the decades that followed the tragedy there has never been any official recognition of the disaster in the Isle of Man. But in 1998 a memorial unveiling ceremony for survivors and relatives took place at Ronaldsway Airport. Emotions were mixed. Many believed that official recognition by the Manx Government came decades too late for some.

Jennifer Curtis (Fleet) unveiling the memorial plaque at Ronaldsway Airport on the 40th anniversary. *(Keigs Photography/Island Photographics)*

It took Elizabeth Moss 40 years to pluck up the courage to visit Winter Hill where her father, Arthur Tonkin died. Arthur Tonkin was just 42 at the time and managing director of Ramsey Motors on the island. On the 40th anniversary she placed a wreath on the hillside in memory of her father who organised the fateful trip. She said:

It is not something that I wanted to do, but it is something I feel I should do. I owe it to my father. I've been planning to come to Winter Hill for many years but I have never had the courage before. I was only a little girl when he died, and I've never really got over it.

I did not think the people of Bolton would be commemorating the 40th anniversary and so the service has come as a complete surprise. I can't tell you how much I appreciate the fact that the victims of the crash are still remembered.

Don Hulme, the Horwich police officer, who helped lay out the bodies in the makeshift mortuary set up in the Victoria Road Methodist Church – whose story is told earlier – would late in his life get to know many of the relatives of those who lost their lives. In 1974, after serving in Farnworth and Liverpool, he transferred to the Isle of Man Constabulary and in the following years worked alongside many of the friends and relatives of those killed. But it wasn't until the 40th anniversary of the disaster that he publicly revealed his involvement. He said: 'I didn't tell anyone on the Isle of Man. I just didn't want to talk about it.' Don retired from the force in 1988 as a Detective Chief Inspector.

Don Hulme as Chief Inspector in 1986. *(Don Hulme)*

Sergeant Bill Brown, the Manx police officer, who travelled over from the Island to identify his father and many of the other victims, returned to Winter Hill 42 years later in the summer of 2000. Accompanied by his son and daughter, they were joined by senior local police officers and an aircraft historian who was able to piece together the last minutes of the flight for them in great detail. Sadly, Bill Brown died the following year.

In 1998 Alan Cretney was the Island's Deputy Chief Constable, he was just 10 when his father was killed in the disaster. John Albert Cretney – known as Jack – was a police sergeant married to Jean. On the day of the tragedy, Jack finished his night shift early so that he could join the party of motor traders. At the time of the 40th anniversary Alan Cretney told the *Isle of Man Examiner* his recollections of that time:

Dad was in the motor patrol, as they called it then. The force was running a Vauxhall, which came from Ramsey Motors, who organised the trip, so he was invited as their guest. He finished his shift at 4 am and came home to get changed and was picked up from the house. I remember seeing him off; it would have been about 7:30 am.

My brother David and I came home from school for lunch. Somebody had been up to see my mum and she told us there had been an accident. At that time I think there were six or seven survivors. What we had to do was listen to the radio every hour, and every half hour we had to go down to the telephone box at the bottom of the road and ring whatever the contact number was. We went to the telephone box together. As the afternoon wore on the survivors were identified, so it was a process of elimination. It would have been about teatime that we knew.

It is all so vividly clear. It has given me a lot of insight in dealing with people who have been involved in tragedies. I know what the other side is like. One of the lessons is that even though it was so long ago it stays in your mind just as vividly. I have a lot of sympathy for families that have suffered trauma. Kids can get into trouble and when you track it back to a tragedy you can understand how it has possibly derailed them.

It was certainly a major blow to the island at the time. I was aware that a lot of people had suffered. Thinking back to that teatime I can remember the house being full of people. It was so confusing. It had taken all afternoon to try and get some information and even by teatime there was still an element of uncertainly.

With this job you learn that people do not always accept the death of a loved one until they have seen the body. If people have died violently and the relatives want to see the body it should always be allowed. I did not see my father's body. A sergeant called Bill Brown went over to Chorley and did the identification. It must have been a terrible ordeal for him. It was probably at the end of the following day, when we got formal confirmation. I don't know how people go on for weeks and weeks not knowing. It must be dreadful.

I have a mental image of standing at the front door and seeing this lime green Vauxhall, which came to pick him up. I can't remember what I did yesterday morning, I'd have to look at my diary, but I remember very clearly standing at the front door that morning. I don't know why I waved him off. I could have been sitting inside eating toast instead. The impact that has made on me is that – always say cheerio. I always do. One moment you see somebody leave the house and you don't know, you might never see him or her again.

Time does not heal it. I think you get used to it, you learn to cope with it. There are not many weeks go by that I do not remember it and every time there is an aircraft accident on television it takes me straight back to some very vivid memories.

We had a lot of support from family and friends, and the police service. There was a formal police funeral and it snowed heavily.

I always wanted to join the police force. David joined the merchant navy and eventually joined the police service and has recently retired. We maintained a tight family relationship. Mum never remarried. I suppose she devoted herself to my brother and me – she died four years ago. There was no back up for the families, no counselling or even compensation and no recognition of posttraumatic stress syndrome. There was a fund set up for the families and each family got about a thousand pounds, which was probably a lot of money in those days.

But you see somebody go and all you get back is a parcel of their belongings. I have still got his watch. It had stopped at twenty to ten.

Even today the tragedy is still remembered in the Lancashire towns of Bolton and Horwich. On Sunday, 25 February 2001, a few days before the 43rd anniversary of the accident, some of those associated with that fateful day braved the icy conditions and assembled at the summit of Winter Hill to attend a poignant open-air remembrance service. Retired Canon Colin Craston, who was the vicar of St Paul's Church, Deansgate, at the time of the crash, paid tribute to those who perished on the hillside and the extraordinary efforts of those who came to help in the aftermath.

Jennifer Curtis who attended the service and the following reception at the Jolly Crofters said:

It does feel very strange to be up here again. I was amazed when I found out that people are still interested in the disaster. I still have very clear memories of the crash and it's something that you can never forget. Winter Hill will always be a place of great sadness for me, as so many families lost loved ones.

Dorothy Howarth (now Asling) travelled from her home in Stafford to pay tribute to her husband Malcolm, who was killed, aged just 25. She said: 'I've relived that day many times and even though it happened so long ago, it still feels as though it was only yesterday.'

Clifford Greenhalgh, now in his seventies, who set out from his home after hearing on the radio the news of the disaster and volunteered to help the emergency services look for survivors, said: 'I saw horrific sights that I will never forget. I'm pleased about today's service because people should remember what happened. It felt very strange being up here again, just yards from where the plane crashed, but it is something I just had to do.'

Rescuer Clifford Greenhalgh returns to Winter Hill on 43rd anniversary.
*(Author's collection)*

# EPILOGUE

*Say not in grief they are no more,*
*But in thankfulness that they were.*

The reader will be aware that I have included very little in the forgoing narrative of the many personal and tragic stories of those who lost friends and relatives in the tragedy. To do so would require a separate volume. However, during my research I came into contact with Sue Somers, who was just seven and a half years old when her father, Arthur Leslie Gleave was killed on Winter Hill. I include her story here in the hope that it gives the reader some insight to the other victims of the disaster – those left behind to grieve and cope in the aftermath of the tragedy. She told me:

My vague recollections on the day of the air disaster are of my mother being worried about him going flying in bad weather – I believe it was thick mist. I don't remember saying goodbye to him either, probably because he must have left the house early before I got up, to make the trip to the airport. I can only recollect a handful of memories of my father up to that day, some good, some bad.

Arthur Gleave. *(Sue Somers)*

He had an allotment near to home where he kept a small mountain of soot to use on the ground. I remember playing in this – I can still smell the soot now when I think of it – seemingly without getting told off. I've learnt later in life what a wicked sense of humour my father had, and that's how I presumably got away

137

with it.

I have an older brother called Michael and another younger called Kevin; they were 9 and 2 respectively at the time. I was always introduced by my father to whomever as 'the jam in the sandwich'. Apparently, being the only girl I was my father's favourite, I could do no wrong; so whatever I did one day to deserve a wrap over the knuckles with a wooden ruler, I can't remember. Mum told me many years later that afterwards, he went straight out to the back kitchen – two rooms away – and sobbed his heart out for disciplining me, he felt dreadful. That's probably one of the last memories I have of my father.

Another memory I have is of going to see him at work after school in his battery shop at Ramsey Motors. He used to sit me on a huge wicker basket, and I can still remember the smell in there from all the batteries, it stunk. He would then drive me home in the firm's van, the sprung seats always squeaked and he would pull my leg by saying I had chickens in my seat – I can still hear them now when I think back. One time driving home, a dog ran out in front of us and was run over, it broke his heart and he cried. Sadly, that's about all I can remember of him.

After the accident happened, my brothers and I were kept away from newspapers, radio and TV coverage, whilst being slipped around between relatives. We all stayed with mum's parents for a while, and that is where mum told us one night, when she was putting us to bed, that dad wouldn't be coming home again …

Teachers at my school were very kind and quiet with me, and very understanding, which was quite the opposite to some of the other children there. One big girl came over to me one day and said: 'You haven't got a daddy have you?' I remember running to my grandparents' house, just across the road from school in tears. I don't remember getting back to normal afterwards.

I do remember being cocooned by my family and my grandparents helping mum bring us up, for example. Mum never got over the loss of dad and she put all her energies into our upbringing.

I was a new mum just turned twenty, when I started grieving for my dad. I tried asking mum questions about him to help me with my 'pictures' in my own head, but I didn't get any indepth information because it upset her so much to talk about it. That left me feeling as if I had only half a childhood, not like other children have. I definitely felt, and still do, that I have missed out on that very important part of my life.

Sue Somers (centre) with her brother and his wife at the memorial unveiling at Ronaldsway Airport.

Bringing up my own family – I have three sons – has, I'm sure, been coloured by my own lacking in my life. When my marriage broke up, my sons were 16, 12 and 9 years old. At the time I found myself going overboard in their care, in all spheres of their lives. I've backed off a lot now because they are all now very strong individual adults, but I was determined they wouldn't feel as if they had lost a parent when we split up because of my own knowledge in that matter. It was very difficult for me putting personal feelings aside concerning their father, but I knew I had to. Their relationship had to be kept open, no matter how he acted – he was an alcoholic – and they did have some difficult and upsetting times with him. Twelve years later he was killed in a motorcycle accident, after he had sorted himself out and got back to a happy loving relationship with each of them. I'm sure they felt it had been worth all the upset at the time and glad they had kept in touch with him. They didn't have the horrible void inside them, as I did, and still do to a point, of disconnection when my father died. They have, if you like, a full movie in their minds, more than I will ever have.

What helps me these days to connect to my dad, and mum – now she has left us too – is my belief that we'll all meet up again one day, that way I don't feel alone. I believe my parents and grandparents look over me and give me guidance, and it feels good. Whether it is true or not doesn't matter. I just need to feel it is.

\*\*\*\*\*\*\*\*\*\*\*\*\*\*\*\*\*\*\*\*\*\*\*\*\*\*\*\*\*

On Winter Hill today the crash scene is desolate and often shrouded in mist; apart from a scar on the hillside there are no visible signs of the crash itself. But if you scrabble around in the peat, as I have done, you will find small pieces of corroded aluminium and rusting rivets from

Charlie Sierra just below the surface. Those are the only few pathetic remains that serve as a poignant reminder of what occurred there nearly half a century ago.

At the nearby transmitter station the original building and glass entrance doors that Bill Howarth staggered through to raise the alarm are still there. The lattice mast of 1958 has since been replaced by a new one at 1,015 feet high, serving both the BBC and ITV, radiating regional and national TV programmes. There are also on the site numerous relays for national and regional FM stereo radio, and a local FM stereo transmitter.

Mounted on the station wall, facing towards the crash site, is a plaque, and anyone passing unaware of the accident can pause for a moment, read in inscription and reflect on what happened on Winter Hill that day. It reads:

## IN MEMORY OF ALL WHO LOST THEIR LIVES AT THE

## WINTER HILL AIR DISASTER 27th FEBRUARY 1958

## AND WITH GRATEFUL THANKS TO THE PEOPLE OF HORWICH AND BOLTON

## FOR THEIR MAGNIFICENT SUPPORT

## ERECTED BY HIS WORSHIP THE MAYOR OF DOUGLAS ISLE OF MAN

## F. KENNISH (SURVIVOR)

## AND THE SURVIVORS, FAMILIES AND FRIENDS OF ALL WHO DIED.

## "SOMEWHERE AROUND THE CORNER ALL IS WELL"

The Winter Hill disaster was, and still is, the worst high ground accident ever to occur in the British Isles. For Silver City Airways it was their first accident involving fatalities in over 200,000 separate flights carrying 1,500,000 passengers in 12 years of operations. The airline was the only independent airline to have been awarded the Cumberbatch Trophy for Air Safety in the British Commonwealth.

Manx Airlines, who operated that charter flight, the accident came right at the end of an historic and memorable 11 years of successful operations. In the spring of 1958 the airlines aircraft and routes were taken over completely by Silver City Airways and the name Manx Airlines disappeared for many years.

There is no doubt that flying today is safer by far than it was in 1958, since then tremendous advances have been made in air safety. Now, nearly 50 years later, aircraft are equipped with modern radar and navigational aids and have the ability to fly above the worst of the weather making another accident in the circumstances leading to the tragic loss of Charlie Sierra almost unthinkable.

But above all the Winter Hill disaster reminds us all of the fragility of life and the fine line technology travels between success and failure. Sadly, as it always is, it took an accident that claimed 35 lives for changes to be made and the introduction of new regulations that should have been in place long before the tragic events of February 1958. As ever, hindsight is a wonderful thing.

But wherever the blame lay for the disaster, there can be no doubt that the people of Bolton and Horwich rose to a difficult rescue operation in appalling conditions with guts, courage and compassion. The dictionary falls short when one seeks a word to describe the untiring efforts of those rescuers, official and unofficial, who struggled through the mist, snow and clinging mud in an attempt to save a few of the 42 lives that had been rudely shattered on the frozen hillside. They themselves would refuse to apply the word 'heroic' to their efforts, but that is the only word, which truthfully covers the situation. They shone like a bright warming light from an otherwise desolate and grim scene. For them, and others in this part of Lancashire, the disaster touched their hearts, and now, nearly 50 years later they are, and always will be inextricably linked to the Manx community.

I hope that this book goes in some way to remember those men who died on that cold and inhospitable hillside on that fateful day the devil cast his net.

**THE END**

# THE SURVIVORS RETURN

Just before this book went to press, the BBC in Manchester, knowing of my interest in the accident, asked for my help in putting together a short documentary on the accident for the North West regional television programme 'Inside Out', which was broadcast in January 2005 – appropriately from the Winter Hill transmitter.

For the last 47 years Mike Cairnes has always wanted to return to Winter Hill to pay his respects and say a final goodbye. So, a few days after Christmas, in a bitter wind and snow showers, a BBC film crew drove Mike up the narrow access road to the transmitter station and landmark mast. He was totally unaware that Jennifer Curtis, his stewardess on that fatal flight, and his rescuers – retired transmitter engineers, Alan Sucksmith and John Hall, were waiting to meet him. None of them had seen each other since that fateful day in 1958. It was a reunion of mixed emotions for them all. In many ways they had all returned to lay some ghosts.

The last word in this story goes to Mike Cairnes. Standing near the crash site, he said: 'Good friends of mine died that day. Over the years I have had many Masses said for them by many priests. What a shame, they were all good people.'

Jennifer Curtis (Fleet) greets Mike Cairnes at the transmitter station - the first time they had seen each other since the day of the crash. *(Bolton Evening News)*

Left to right - Mike Cairnes, Alan Sucksmith, John Hall, Jennifer Curtis (Fleet). *(Bolton Evening News)*

# THE PASSENGERS AND CREW

| | |
|---|---|
| Thomas Adams | Norman Ennett (Survivor) |
| John Bridson | Arthur Gleave |
| Norman H Brown | Thomas Gilbertson |
| W. R. Cain | David Harding |
| Ralph Caine | Bill Harding |
| Mike Cairnes (Survivor) | Bill Howarth (Survivor) |
| Edward Christian | Malcolm Howarth |
| Thomas Arthur Callow | Leslie Stuart Kneale |
| Ray Clague | Selwyn Lace |
| Robert Corkill | Frank Leece |
| Daniel Charles Corlett | James Howard Lindsay |
| William Neville Corlett | Fred Kennish (Survivor) |
| George William Corlett | Victor James McMahon |

Louis Cowin

John Douglas Craine

William Crellin

John Crennell

Jack Cretney

Thomas James Crosbie (Survivor)

Jennifer Curtis – now Fleet (Survivor)

John Wade Farger

William Russell Moore

Jack Parkes

Edward Partington

Charles Edward Staley

Arthur Tonkin

Thomas Alma Watts

Thomas Williams

Harold Williamson
(Survivor)

# MANX AIRLINES

Formed as Manx Air Charters in May 1947, as an associate company of Air Charter Experts, also based at Ronaldsway, they began operations with two Dragon Rapides. Flying out of Ronaldsway, Manx Air Charters undertook passenger and freight charters to the north of England, Scotland and Northern Ireland.

For the 1948 season, five Dragon Rapides were in service and in July Air Charter Experts closed down and their charter commitments were transferred to Manx Air Charters. Both 1948 and 1949 were busy seasons for the airline, but in 1949 competition arose when a new Isle of Man based company, North West Airlines began scheduled services from Ronaldsway.

In 1950, an application for a BEA Associate Agreement was made for a scheduled service from the Isle of Man to Carlisle, a route formerly operated by Northern Air Charter and Mannin Airways. Approval was given for a summer-only service operating between May and September. This scheduled service was only a small part of Manx's operations, but the success of this route laid down the foundations of Manx's future scheduled services.

The Rapides continued to operate their many charter flights from the island and the company under took several air ambulance flights. The Rapides could be quickly converted to take a stretcher and urgent cases could then be flown from the island to hospitals on the mainland.

At the end of the 1952 season, North West Airlines ceased operations. This closure of its rival, coupled with the relaxation of the laws regulating the operation of scheduled services by private airlines, meant that Manx Air Charters could look forward to a bright and prosperous future.

In 1953, Manx Air Charters applied for scheduled services from Ronaldsway to Newcastle and Renfrew. These routes were approved and in February 1953 the company changed its name to Manx Airlines. The Rapides were retained and two 34-seat Dakotas entered service for use on the lucrative Glasgow route. The Dakotas were also used on the service to Newcastle when loads were heavy, and they were also available for charter work during the quiet winter months.

The introduction of the Dakotas, and of the new scheduled routes, was soon reflected in the company's passenger figures. During 1951 and 1952, the combined passenger total for both years was 11,569, while the 1953 total alone soared to 14,881. A staff of only 27 people, including five captains, achieved this figure. Most of these passengers were carried on the run to Glasgow, which was flown daily, even during the winter. The 1954 passenger figures were even better than those returned in 1953, with a total of 21,436 passengers being carried by the airline.

The Dakotas were often used for charter work carrying freight and newspapers to the Isle of Man and other charters took the aircraft to Europe. It was on one of those European trips that disaster struck. On 22 December 1955, a Manx Airlines Dakota, G-AMZC, crashed on the approach to land at Dusseldorf airport, killing the three crew members. This left Manx with one Dakota and three Rapides for the 1956 season.

However, before the season got underway, the British Aviation Services group bought out Manx Airlines in May. Manx Airlines, although continuing to operate under its own name, became part of the Northern Division of Silver City Airways. Two Bristol Wayfarers were transferred by Silver City to its Manx associate, and these aircraft were flown throughout the summer on the routes to Glasgow and Newcastle, while the Rapides continued to fly on the run to Carlisle. With the introduction of the Wayfarers the one remaining Dakota was transferred to Silver City.

In 1957 a third Bristol Wayfarer was added to the Manx fleet and two DH Herons were loaned from Silver City Airways. In May of that year a route from Ronaldsway to Belfast was opened in addition to the services to Carlisle, Glasgow and Newcastle.

Right at the end of 11 years of memorable service came the tragic loss of the Wayfarer on Winter Hill and very soon after the name Manx Airlines disappeared as its aircraft and routes were integrated with those of Silver City Airways.

Wayfarers on the apron at Ronaldsway. *(Terry Faragher collection)*

# SILVER CITY AIRWAYS

Silver City's operations were not confined to the transportation of cars across the Channel, indeed they covered nearly every sphere of aviation.

It all began in November 1945 with the formation of British Aviation Services Ltd and the appointment of Air Commodore Griffith Powell as its Chairman. He was considered an ideal candidate given his pre-war position as a pilot with Imperial Airways and a distinguished career as Senior Staff Officer with No. 5 Group Royal Air Force Transport Command at Montreal, Canada. It was his expertise in long-range ferry operations across the Atlantic that formed the basis for the new company.

They established their offices in Great Cumberland Place, London and one of the first jobs involved the delivery of five Short Sandringham Flying Boats to Buenos Aires in December.

The company located its maintenance base at Blackbushe employing some of the finest engineers available at the time. 'Taffy' Powell's experience with 45 Group enabled him to select the best aircrew available for these arduous ferry crossings and this gave great standing to British Aviation Services in those post-war years. The list was impressive and included Captain D. Fenton AFC, H. Banting and H. Graham AFC who held the record of five and a half hours for a transatlantic crossing in a DH Mosquito from Gander to Prestwick.

Their first major contract was to ferry 36 ex-RAF C-47s from Silloth to Montreal for conversion for the post-war civil market and their eventual delivery.

The new company was registered in the United Kingdom as an airline company on 25 November 1946. The board of directors consisted of W. Robinson, J. Govett and 'Taffy' Powell. With a nominated capital of £500,000 they were able to set up the operation and purchase seven aircraft: three Avro Lancastrians including spares direct from the manufacturer, and four Douglas C-47s from the US Foreign Liquidation Commission. The financial backing was provided by a group of Australian and British mining companies and its main purpose was to provide a regular air service between the UK and the companies' interests overseas. Other senior personnel included the Company Secretary Lawrence Barnes, Accountant Bill Menzies, Personnel Manager John Whittemore, Chief Pilot Len Madelaine and the Chief Engineer was Sydney Tennett. The name Silver City Airways was chosen because Broken Hill in New South Wales was the Zinc Corporation's mining territory and the town had been named the 'Silver City'.

The first operation took place at the end of November with regular flights between the UK, South Africa and Australia using Avro Lancastrians on behalf of the Zinc Corporation until 1948. They also undertook the delivery of many surplus aircraft to foreign Air Forces as well as those for new civilian operators. In conjunction with this they purchased a Lockheed Lodestar in order to return their aircrews to the UK.

In October 1947, Silver City leased a Bristol Freighter from the Bristol Aeroplane Company and along with four Dakotas they took part in the movement of displaced refugees following the partition of India. The Bristol Freighter was equipped with long-range fuel tanks placed inside the fuselage. The aircraft had no seats fitted and the passengers had to sit on the floor of the freighter along with their luggage. This aircraft carried 1,105 refugees in just nine days of flying. It was the versatility of this aircraft on these mercy flights that resulted in 'Taffy' Powell developing its use for the Car Ferry Service.

On 14 July 1947, Bristol Freighter G-AGVC under the command of Captain Storm Clark and First Officer Jerry Rosser took off from Lympne on the first revenue charter to Le Touquet on what was to become Silver City's most famous route that would last for over 23 years. Although the cost of 32 was more expensive than the sea ferries the time saved ensured instant success for the airline. In addition they undertook a variety of general freight charters as well as regular horse and livestock charter to and from the Continent.

In September 1948, they sent four Bristol Freighters to Hamburg to assist in the Berlin Airlift and although their presence was short lived on this occasion they continued to operate there on and off until 1953.

They also ran a small fleet of aircraft that were fitted out in a VIP configuration and these carried many distinguished people including Winston Churchill on several occasions.

In 1950 they set up a French subsidiary company to operate on the cross Channel services in conjunction with Silver City as a way of placating the French authorities – nothing new there then!

In March 1953 they bought out the last UK flying boat operator Aquila Airways but they continued to operate under their own name until they ceased operations in 1958.

April 1953 saw the introduction of the new Mk32 Bristol Superfreighter with a 50% increase in capacity resulting in reduced fares and increased frequency on the car ferry services. The year 1953 also saw the takeover of another Kent based operator, the very successful Air Kruise run by Hugh and Audrey Kennard. They specialised in scheduled and charter flights to the Continent using Dragon Rapides from Lympne and Ramsgate. They continued to operate under their own name until they were absorbed into the parent company in 1958. They added further to the success of the company with the introduction of their inclusive tour services or as we know them now – the package holiday. The company also introduced the first road-rail-air service linking London and Paris.

Silver City maintained a group of jet-trained aircrew that were available to deliver military aircraft on behalf of the manufacturers. In June 1953 Captain Johnnie Hackett and First Officer Pete Moneypenny delivered the first of several English Electric Canberras to South America for the Venezuelan Air Force.

A Silver City Airways Bristol Freighter being readied for flight.

In 1954 Silver City financed the construction of the first new civilian airport to be built in the UK since the war. It was built on the Romney Marsh in Kent near the small village of Lydd and named Ferryfield to reflect the nature of its operation and it remains in operation to this day. By the end of 1954 they were operating services from Lydd as well as Southampton and London Gatwick to destinations in the Channel Islands as well as Calais, Le Touquet and Ostend. In 1955 they extended their sphere of operation to include services from Stranraer and Blackpool to Northern Ireland and the Isle of Man.

One notable operation that Silver City were involved in at the end of 1956 was the airlift of Hungarian refugees from Austria to Blackbushe, using two Dakotas borrowed from Air Kruise. When the airlift came to an end in December Silver City and Air Kruise had flown a total of 26 round trips carrying over 800 people out of Austria.

Since 1953 Silver City had been operating in Libya and were responsible for the formation of Libyan Airlines establishing an operating base at Tripoli. As Libya opened to the outside world so its oil assets were being developed by the likes of BP and Total oil. Silver City played a big part in these operations until they finally left in 1961.

During the lifetime of the company they were called upon on several occasions to supply aircraft and crews for filming including a sequence at Wolverhampton where a Bristol Freighter suffered a brake failure during the making of a 'Man in the Sky', slewing off the runway and ending up in a ditch.

In 1956, Silver City Airways' parent company, British Aviation Services, bought out the Lancashire Aircraft Corporation and Manx Airlines. These companies eventually amalgamated to form the Northern Division of Silver City Airways based in Blackpool. Several of Silver City's Bristol Wayfarers were transferred to the Lancashire Aircraft Corporation and Manx Airlines, and in February 1957 the company bought two Herons to augment the Wayfarer fleet. The names of the Lancashire Aircraft Corporation and Manx Airlines were kept alive until October 1957 when they were dropped, and all the aircraft were painted in the Silver City Airways' livery. The final piece of the Northern Division jigsaw fell into place in 1957 with the purchase of Dragon Airways from Hunting Clan giving them another operation base, this time at Newcastle.

The parent company, Britavia had purchased a fleet of Handley Page Hermes from BOAC in 1954 and they used them mainly on Ministry contracts, but in 1959 they were transferred to Silver City and operated the Silver Arrow rail-air link between Manston and Le Touquet. Although these long-range aircraft were operated by BOAC, Silver City became the first operator to fly a Hermes across the North Atlantic.

In 1955 Silver City were honoured with the Cumberbatch Trophy, the British Commonwealth's highest safety award. No accident had marred its record since operations began. But, on 1 November 1961 tragedy struck when Bristol Superfreighter, G-ANWL overshot the runway at Guernsey, and in attempting to go round again struck the ground with a wing tip. The aircraft cartwheeled and broke in two. The front section caught fire and the two pilots were killed. Fortunately the seven passengers and steward on board escaped from the aircraft without serious injury. This was Silver City's first fatal accident in more than 250,000 cross-Channel flights since July 1948.

On 23 January 1962, it was announced that the shareholders of British Aviation Services had agreed to exchange their shares for Air Holdings stock. Air Holdings had originally been founded in November 1961 to act as the holding company for British United Airways. Because of this merger Silver City became part of British United Airways in January 1962. By January 1963 their services had been fully integrated into the service schedule of British United and the name Silver City Airways disappeared. However, the car ferry service was to continue with Bristol Superfreighters and the newly introduced Aviation Traders Carvair until the final car ferry service took place in January 1971 between Lydd and Le Touquet.

Few airlines that emerged in the post-war years were as colourful, pioneering and successful as Silver City, and its role in the development of post-war British air transport has become legendary. There now exists a Silver City Association that charts their history and keeps in contact with ex aircrew and staff, all of whom had a tremendous affection for the airline.